D1452781

Studies in the Gospel from China

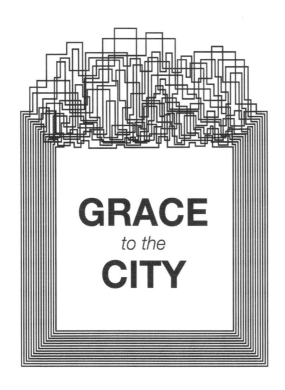

GRACE
*to the*
CITY

Edited by
S. E. Wang and
Hannah Nation

CHINA PARTNERSHIP

# ontents

# Foreword

Twenty-five years ago, as I was finishing seminary, I came to a fork in the road. Would I continue to pursue pastoral ministry after graduating or try my hand at doctoral studies? When I started seminary, I had two goals – to do well in school and then serve the Lord as a pastor. But two events changed everything: a trip and a prayer.

As one of the pastoral interns, I was asked to lead a group of college students on a short-term mission trip to visit a missionary in Indonesia that our church supported. We went to visit him and learn about his work, which was a combination of serving as a seminary professor and assisting with local church planting. As I observed him mentoring and discipling future pastoral leaders for the church in Indonesia, I saw the exponential influence he was having on gospel work in that country. This trip stirred my heart, so I began to pray.

I prayed seeking to discern this strange feeling in my heart. Why was his work as a professor training future pastors so compelling? So, I prayed for wisdom. In addition to praying with my wife, I asked others, including my parents and mentors to pray with me. As the days turned into weeks, I began to sense a deep burden and desire in my heart to do something similar to what he was doing, namely, training future pastors and leaders, especially in a place that did not have educational resources that we had in the United States.

## Foreword

So, with the encouragement of my wife, parents, and professors, I began to sense a call to further my education so I could become a missionary teacher, serving the church in a country with limited theological resources. In addition to this new career trajectory, my wife and I also started to pray about which area of the world would be a good fit. It didn't take long for both of us to sense a call to pray for China. We didn't know what this might mean for our future, but we continued to pray and trust the Lord. We were convinced God was sovereignly directing our paths and that whatever the Lord opened up, we would obey.

Now, we did not end up going to China as missionaries. But I did become a teacher of future pastors. When I was finishing my PhD studies, I received an invitation to serve at the seminary where I had received my master's degree. While at first I was hesitant to serve here in the United States, I learned quickly that the work that I would be doing, namely, training pastoral leaders to serve the world, could just as well be accomplished in the United States.

So, for the last twenty years I have served the Lord by teaching students not only from the United States, but from around the world, including China. I was convinced that part of my job was to help them to see that wherever the Lord called them, they should earnestly desire to make disciples of all nations. In fact, because of my previous burden for China, I have made several trips there, teaching pastoral leaders. I also had the immense privilege of meeting several of the authors in this volume, listening and learning about their lives and their ministries.

One of the lasting impressions that these pastors left with me was their unbridled hope in God. In spite of past trials and present challenges, they possessed a single-minded hope in the gospel of grace and what it could do in the lives of their people and country. In my travels to China over the last 10 years, I have been so encouraged to see God's sovereign hand in these faithful pastors and churches.

I began to ask, Could it be that after decades of being a "closed country" to the gospel, China would experience an outpouring of the Holy Spirit? Could it be that a movement based upon the gospel of grace would ignite hearts and establish churches? Could it be that as gospel-centered, grace-driven, mission-minded churches are established, the center of Christianity will shift from the west and the north to the global east and the south? If so, I believe this book represents just a small part of what we in the West need to do now: listen to, learn from, and partner with our brothers and sisters in China.

My prayer is that the Spirit of God will continue to pour out his blessings upon not just the church in China, but the global church, that as we see both the triumphs and trials of God's family worldwide, we would not only be able to rejoice with those who rejoice, but also weep with those who weep. Furthermore, it is my earnest prayer that our vision of what constitutes "real Christianity" would be sharpened by what we are seeing in the global church, especially in places like China. May our hearts and minds be stirred to pray that God's name would be exalted among all the nations and

# Foreword

out his blessings upon not just the church in China, but the global church, that as we see both the triumphs and trials of God's family worldwide, we would not only be able to rejoice with those who rejoice, but also weep with those who weep. Furthermore, it is my earnest prayer that our vision of what constitutes "real Christianity" would be sharpened by what we are seeing in the global church, especially in places like China. May our hearts and minds be stirred to pray that God's name would be exalted among all the nations and that every knee will bow and every tongue confess that Jesus Christ is Lord.

Maranatha, come Lord Jesus.

Rev. Julius J. Kim, PhD
President, The Gospel Coalition
Escondido, California
October 2020

# Preface

Today it is easy to find many people writing *about* the church in China, analyzing its theological positions and social impact. It is much more difficult to find the actual gospel voice of the Chinese church—the sermons, prayers, and beliefs of the people themselves.

This project aims to step away from delivering thoughts about the Chinese house church and instead offer the English-speaking world a chance to sit directly at the feet of our Chinese brothers and sisters. It is time for us to stop simply observing what is taking place in China. It is time for us to start allowing Chinese Christians to lead us to Christ, to start learning from and listening to the fresh outpouring of the Holy Spirit taking place in their country.

The initial theological canon of the urban, 21st century Chinese house church is forming. This makes now an important time to ensure its leading voices are heard by the global church. As a grace-centered understanding of the gospel impacts the traditional house church, many of China's pastors are developing a rich theological perspective that is both uniquely Chinese and rooted in the historic doctrines of the Reformed faith. Throughout its history, Chinese culture has invested deeply in scholarship and contemplation; as Christianity engages the heart of this ancient society, we anticipate increased development of China's theological vision.

# Preface

At China Partnership, we are blessed to have unique access to the sermons and writing of a gospel movement taking place in many of China's house churches today. Our desire is to help global Christians hear and learn from the voice of the Chinese house church. We are privileged to stand on the shoulders of other leading voices looking at and studying the broader Chinese church. Through others' efforts, the ground is fertile for projects such as this that translate and publish Chinese house church theology. What makes this project unique is our belief that the Chinese pastors involved in a movement called 恩典城市 ("Grace to City") have something to say directly to Western churches and a role to play in teaching and reviving our spirituality. It is our privilege to help contribute their voice to the global conversation on faith.

Will the Western church revive? Only the Lord knows. But just as the spiritual life and vitality of the European Reformation relied in part on the sharing and dissemination of theological resources through translation, print, and media in order for the good news of grace to cross linguistic barriers and cultural divisions, it is my conviction that revival in the Western church will in part rely on our ability and willingness to be taught by those churches currently experiencing an abundant outpouring of the Holy Spirit.

Today the Chinese house church is the fastest-growing church on the planet. If we want revival in the West, we should begin by listening to those currently being revived. May we have eyes to see and ears to hear.

# A Note on Using this Book

In this book are five essays developed from talks given by leading voices in the Reformed house church movement: Wang Yi, Simon Liu, Peng Qiang, Gao Zhen, and Yang Xibo. Because its content was developed from sermons, it is not academic in nature; rather, it is pastoral in its emphasis and tone. Of course, it is also a resource for understanding the growing gospel movement within the Chinese house church, but we hope that readers outside of China will be ministered to and experience similar revival and renewal.

This book contains five studies on the gospel of grace, each concluding with a prayer from the author and a short reflection guide. The reflection questions are intended to help readers engage the content either for personal devotional use or group study. We believe this book can provide fruitful conversations for anyone preparing for ministry internationally or seeking to better relate to the global church, as well as Sunday school classes or small groups discussing the history of the church and its modern-day realities.

However you engage this book and consider the rich theology driving the renewal of the Chinese house church, we urge you to unite your spirits together in prayer with your brothers and sisters. The Chinese house church is marked and identified by its commitment to prayer. Ask any of the pastors featured in this book how to bless their churches, and they will without hesitation request committed and regular prayer on their behalf.

## Preface

For some, there are real stakes for bearing the name of Christ. All of the pastors who lead Grace to the City have at times been arrested, some frequently. But for all Christians in China, the mundane and daily task of picking up one's cross to follow Christ looks similar to the social pressures, family stresses, and burdensome temptations faced by those in the West. You are not unfamiliar with the things that press your brothers and sisters hard from every side.

Will you join them now before the throne of grace?

A special and deeply felt thank you to Jason Chen, Moses Han, J. Cha, and Ryan Zhang for their faithful and dedicated translation of the original materials, and also to E. F. Gregory for her editing assistance. We praise the Lord for this use of your many gifts.

Hannah Nation

# 1

# Grace Reigns

## Wang Yi

*Wang Yi was a well-known constitutional law scholar at Chengdu University for many years, and one of the top scholars in the liberal wing of a movement that tried to bring constitutionalism and rule of law to China. Then he was converted to Christianity.*

*As a writer, he has been moving from approaching everything as a political leader to approaching things as a pastor. The dominating consideration for him today is the eschatological centrality and importance of the church, and a main thrust in his thinking is the theology of the cross. He is a passionate visionary and a humble learner.*

*Wang Yi was arrested in December 2018 under the Chinese government's new religious regulations; his "unregistered" house church, Early Rain Covenant Church, had hundreds of members and was meeting openly in the city of Chengdu. As of this writing he is in prison serving a term of 9 years.*

For sin indeed was in the world before the law was given, but sin is not counted where there is no law. Yet death reigned from Adam to Moses, even over those whose sinning was not like the transgression of Adam, who was a type of the one who was to come.

But the free gift is not like the trespass. For if many died through one man's trespass, much more have the grace of God and the free gift by the grace of that one man Jesus Christ abounded for many. And the free gift is not like the result of that one man's sin. For the judgment following one trespass brought condemnation, but the free gift following many trespasses brought justification. For if, because of one man's trespass, death reigned through that one man, much more will those who receive the abundance of grace and the free gift of righteousness reign in life through the one man Jesus Christ.

Therefore, as one trespass led to condemnation for all men, so one act of righteousness leads to justification and life for all men. For as by the one man's disobedience the many were made sinners, so by the one man's obedience the many will be made righteous. Now the law came in to increase the trespass, but where sin increased, grace abounded all the more, so that, as sin reigned in death, grace also might reign through righteousness leading to eternal life through Jesus Christ our Lord.

Romans 5:13–21

## Wang Yi

A countryman from the Tang Dynasty wrote this classic poem on his way to the north:

> "Ahead, I see no ancient sages,
> nor behind, those sages yet unborn.
> While, on and on, heaven and earth shall roll, alone I stand, tears a-falling, forlorn."

This poem mentions two people: one in the past, another coming in the future. If you do not see these two, you will live a hopeless life of wandering and solitude.

I want to use Romans 5 to interpret this classic poem by Chen Zi'ang. His lament is rare in Chinese culture. He is filled with what we modern people call "ultimate concern" for the universe, history, and life. But the question remains: whom does he really want to meet? Who is this person that is able to satisfy the historic purpose of the infinite universe? This person would bring purpose to the author's life and wipe away his tears of loneliness and sorrow. Who on earth could he be?

In Romans 5, Paul answers Chen Zi'ang's question. According to Paul's answer, I can make a few changes to the famous poem:

> "Ahead, I see no Adam, nor behind, I see no Christ.
> While, on and on, heaven and earth shall roll, alone I stand, tears a-falling, for-lorn."

I praise the Lord, because his gospel has come to China and to us.

The cross of Jesus has rescued us from the despair and hopelessness of an infinite heaven and universe. We have seen Christ and his cross on Golgotha. He split open the rock for us with his blood. Through it, he leads us into the Holy of Holies, into the presence of God the Father, so that we might receive adoption as sons. Through the apostle John, he leads us to see the future of the whole world and the final one who is to come and sit on the throne: that is himself, our Lord Jesus, the lamb who was slain.

Now Adam has passed. Christ will come again. Reflecting on an infinite heaven and earth, believers in Christ should rise up and worship, turning our weeping into tears of joy. Therefore, Paul says that what reigns over us today is no longer death, but life. It is no longer Adam's sin, but Christ's righteousness. The law is no longer king; rather grace is king. Amen!

Let us focus on two things. First, let us meet the people of the past. Second, let us meet the One to come. I will use Martin Luther and John Calvin's interpretation of Romans 5:20–21 to demonstrate the gospel of grace. Then I will ask the Lord to show us through these two verses the One who is to come: Christ, the Son of the living God.

## The Prognosis

In Romans 5, Paul repeatedly contrasts Adam with Christ. In these repeated contrasts between Adam and Christ, Paul raises two opposite principles. Paul is asking us who reigns in our lives. What is governing us? Paul identifies that which reigned in Adam three times in verses 14, 17, and 21. In verse 14, death reigned from Adam to Moses. In verse 17, death reigned through one man, Adam. In verse 21, sin reigned in death. Both Luther and Calvin point out that as Paul makes his contrast in this passage, his word choice is casual, and his structure is not very organized.

Does death reign, or does sin reign? Paul uses these two words interchangeably. He emphasizes that in human society after Adam's fall, man is no longer his own master but is governed by his sin. Once man sinned, he is no longer able to stay away from it. Once he sinned the first time, he cannot stop doing it, because what reigns now is not human will and intention but the power of sin and its fruit, death.

Verse 13 says, "Sin indeed was in the world before the law was given." Sin is too crafty for the law to take hold of it. Luther quotes Augustine, saying directly that the law cannot take sin away. Sin is so heavy that the law cannot carry it. Have you ever seen someone hauling a truck with a bicycle? Likewise, the law cannot haul our sin. Paul is saying that the purpose of the law is not to carry away sin. It simply cannot. The purpose of the law is to reveal sin. Since Adam, we sinners have lost everything; we deserve nothing.

From this perspective, death reigned from Adam to Moses. This does not mean that death no longer reigned after Moses. Death will continue to reign till the end of this old world. But before Moses, mankind did not know the reason death reigned in their lives. In other words, before the law was given to the Israelites, not only did death reign, but people were kept in the dark as to why. Without the law, there was no way to know sin and its power and the miserable conditions under sin's reign.

The law reveals sin to men. After Moses received the law on Mount Sinai, the Israelites discovered the fact that death reigns in sinners. This discovery did not change the fact that death reigned. But this discovery made sinners aware of sin and their hopelessness, which made them more conscious of their misery.

So, Paul makes a series of contrasts: sin reigns, grace reigns, death reigns, righteousness reigns. You must focus on Paul's main point, "What we lost in Adam, we regain in Christ." Not only that, but what we regain outweighs what we lost. As verse 15 says, the free gift is not like the trespass.

Paul uses two terms to describe the grace of Christ. Here I call them "royal grace" and "abundant grace." The first tells us that grace comes from the king; the second, that grace is greater than all of our sin. Grace is a reward from a superior to an inferior. There is no grace between those who are equal. There are only responsibilities and the rights of equals. Absolute inequality leads to absolute grace, because inequality means the inferior has no right to demand, and the superior has no responsibility to give. We have no right to demand, and God has no responsibility to give anything except for death. We must understand this premise before we can understand grace.

After Paul clarifies the gospel of grace, he uses Romans 11:35 to explain the meaning of royal grace. He says, "Who has given a gift to him that he might be repaid?" Grace means you must recognize that the one who grants you grace is the king. If Christ were not the king who reigns over you and has the right to demand anything of you, the cross of Christ would not be considered grace. You must also recognize that the one who forgives you is the one who has the right to destroy you. The one who judges you is the one who can throw you into hell. If Christ does not have the right to destroy you, then his forgiveness cannot be considered forgiveness. This is the first reason trespasses cannot surpass free grace, because grace comes from the king. The king can deliver judgment or show mercy, but his grace outweighs his judgment.

Let us take an example from the secular world: amnesty is greater than a guilty verdict. Forgiving someone and judging someone are contradictory, for one says to kill him, the other says not to kill him. If you hold both documents in the same hand, the amnesty to forgive is more effective than the verdict to kill. This is what royal grace means; free grace is not like the trespass.

Forgiveness comes from the king, and the command to forgive can come even before the command to judge. In the *Water Margin*, one of the four classic Chinese novels, there is a man named Chai Jin whose family holds a death-exemption medal bestowed by the emperor. If he commits a crime punishable by death, he can take out this medal and be exonerated. That is to say, there is an amnesty granted to the descendants of his family even before they commit crime, and this amnesty is more effective than any judgment. I read the *Water Margin* when I was a child, and my most ridiculous, unrealistic daydream was to have a death-exemption medal so that whatever felonies I committed in the future, I would be protected my whole life long.

When I got married I was not yet a believer. I had an agreement with my wife that if she ever felt that I treated her well and thus deserved her lifelong kindness, she would give me a death-exemption medal. If I then got in trouble and she was angry with me, I could pull out this death-exemption medal, and she would have to forego the right to judge and punish me. She would have to forgive me. And vice versa.

One time we got into a huge fight, almost to the point of getting a divorce. At that time, I still had in my hand two death-exemption medals from her, and she had three from me. But our death-exemption certificates were all worthless papers, because they were not issued by the king who was nailed to the cross. They were issued by us. At the time, I did not know that sin and death reigned over us. Sinners are not able to preemptively forgive the offenses and harms of others. It was in that year, shortly after our death-exemption medals lost effect with each other, that Christ's death-exemption came to us. Christ's cross fulfilled my childhood daydream.

The law is the verdict; grace is the death-exemption medal. The law cannot take away sin because sin existed before the law. Therefore, Luther summarizes that the law cannot give us life. For as Paul says, "The law came in to increase the trespass."

Luther quotes Augustine again, saying the law will reveal that those who think they can fulfill the law by their own efforts will be more enslaved by the chains of sin. Why? There is a type of rope that grows tighter the more you try to escape from it. In a different classical Chinese novel, *Journey to the West*, the crown on the Monkey King's brow is a perfect example of this ethical shackling.[1] Luther gives another example: if a doctor comes to visit a patient and gives him a prognosis, saying he is terminally ill and there is no treatment, we can say that the doctor's presence actually increases the patient's hopelessness and despair, thereby aggravating his condition. Sometimes the patient hates the doctor because the doctor delivers the worst possible news.

Calvin also helps us understand why the law not only fails to remove sin but actually increases it. He argues that according to Paul, God lets men recognize that sin reigns in them and that death results from the corruption of this reigning sin. Men without the law are like sinking ships; although they are doomed for destruction, they can still survive for a while. Maybe before the ship goes down, they can still get one more divorce, marry one more time, or take a second mortgage for another house. Therefore, in order to demonstrate the greatness of salvation beyond all human

---

1. Whenever the monkey is disobedient, his teacher recites a spell to tighten the crown as a way to punish him.

expectation, the Lord waited until the last moment before the water swallowed humanity and they were sinking into despair. The law was given so that those who had already been judged would be condemned again.

Legalism uses the law, or certain external, visible attempts to obey the law, in our lives as evidence of being saved from the sinking ship. Legalism keeps coming back.

In our contemporary culture, legalism can return in the form of religious individualization, internalization of faith, or moral religiosity. We do not understand that justification by the law is the exact reason the ship of humanity is sinking at an accelerated speed. We do not understand that justification by the law is more evil and more detestable to God than any specific violation of the law because it directly contradicts the reason why the law was given.

The Jews did not understand why the law was given. Sadly, many Christians in the church today still do not know why the law was given. As Paul puts it, it is to imprison everyone under sin to increase the trespass so that God may have mercy on all.

In Calvin's words, God's sole purpose for giving the law was to cut off our hope of self-justification. It is like cutting off alcohol for the drunkard or tobacco for a chain smoker. In this sense, the purpose of the law and the purpose of the gospel are exactly the same. The common goal for the law and the gospel is to cut off all hope of justification outside of the cross of Jesus Christ. It frees our value, identity, and dignity from the law. We can no longer rely on our own behavior.

The law reveals our addiction. We are addicted to declaring ourselves righteous, addicted to moral self-reliance, addicted to distinguishing ourselves by being good people. We are addicted to mediocre self-evaluation. Moralism makes us addicted to our own righteousness, and only the gospel can cut off this addiction. This is not to deny the goodness of the law or of ethics but rather to snatch the goodness of the law and ethics back from our impure, sinful nature and shameful self-evaluation. It forbids us from using our own name to take away any merit that can only be attributed to Jesus.

Moralism makes us addicted to our own righteousness, and only the gospel can cut off this addiction. This is not to deny the goodness of the law or of ethics but rather to snatch the goodness of the law and ethics back from our impure, sinful nature and shameful self-evaluation. It forbids us from using our own name to take away any merit that can only be attributed to Jesus.

## Christ the King

Paul next describes a condition that directly contradicts the reign of sin and death: the reign of grace. Verse 21 is the last contrast between Adam and Christ in chapter 5. Death reigns through Adam's sin; grace reigns through Christ's righteousness.

Luther reminds us that Paul made a distinction between grace and the gift of grace. Luther says that "the gift" in Paul's words is the righteousness given to us. Because of Christ's work and God's pleasure with Christ, God graciously gives us his righteousness. It takes work to remove sin, and with work comes gifts. Christ's work produces the gift, which is able to remove sin. The reason the law cannot remove sin is because the law itself does not have anything to give man. Only Christ's righteousness can be granted to those who believe in him.

Verse 21 says this gift is eternal life. Thus, the gospel of Christ signifies a new kind of reign: in contrast to "death reigns," now "eternal life reigns." In contrast to "sin reigns," in the gospel, "righteousness reigns." Both Calvin and Luther again point out that Paul is not confined by strict logical correspondence. Grace becomes the way Christ reigns.

Yes, your God reigns. Christ has power over this planet. Before Jesus Christ comes back again on that formidable day, grace is the way Christ the king reigns in this evil world and leads his church. It is a primary principle, a new law, and a new covenant. This is what it means for grace to reign.

Romans 5 is the turning point of the entire book. For the rest of Romans, Paul describes only those who live under grace, meaning he is only describing us. That is to say, starting in Romans 6:1, the principle of "grace reigns" is portrayed as being "under grace" as opposed to "under law." Romans 6:12 says the consequence of living under grace is that sin can no longer reign in our bodies. Grace requires us to cast away the power of sin in order that the body of sin might be brought to nothing. At the same time, grace promises us that even though sin still exists, for those of us who live under grace, sin no longer reigns. Grace means that God has given us a death-exemption medal. Because the Lord Jesus died for us, we are exempt from death in the future.

"Grace reigns" demonstrates the promise of the gospel itself, the power of the gospel, and the primary principle of the Christian life. For Christians, grace becomes the motivation for life and the governing principle. For example, Paul urges Timothy, "My child, be strengthened by the grace that is in Christ Jesus." Paul is not saying you are too weak; you are despised for your youth, so be strengthened by the law. Paul knows that a person can only be strengthened by grace; without grace one can only be hardened. Acts 13 gives us another example. Many Jews and devout converts to Judaism followed Paul and Barnabas. The two spoke with them and urged them to continue in the grace of God. They did not urge them to continue in the law of God, because the secret of sanctification is not in striving to obey the law but rather in abiding in the grace of God.

Gratitude is now the only acceptable, legal motivation for sanctification. Any other ethical motivations are evil, as they will all lead us away from the cross of Jesus Christ to obey the law. Gratitude has to be, must be, and will definitely be the consequence of continuing in the grace of God. This is what the reign of grace means.

Grace now motivates us and helps us live a holy life. The law is the steering wheel, and grace is the gas pedal. In a car without gas, even with the best techniques, you can only pretend to be driving. The essence of moralism is pretending to be driving, something which many people have been doing for decades. Although sanctification is a lifelong battle between the flesh and the Spirit, and although Christians will fall seven times, weep a hundred times, and sin a thousand times, grace means that from now on a true believer can be called "conqueror" because he has a death-exemption medal forged by the precious blood of Jesus Christ.

This is my summary: the world after the cross of Jesus is a world where grace reigns.

When Martin Luther passed away, his last words were, "We are beggars. This is true." The reign of grace not only means that the one who gives us grace must be king, but it also means that the one who receives grace must be a beggar. We can define a beggar as someone who admits he lives only at the mercy of others. Is this not the definition of a Christian, my brothers and sisters? To believe in Jesus means that, morally, we have to admit that we are beggars. This is the same from the moment of baptism until the moment of death.

Only a beggar can be totally governed by grace. Only a beggar will totally accept the authority of grace. A beggar completely entrusts his destiny and his next meal to the behavior of other people. The same goes for us. We entrust our souls and eternal destiny to the gospel of Jesus Christ and him crucified.

As one theologian says, the gospel of grace reigning means that between our personal behavior and our final salvation, there is no unbreakable, irreversible causal relationship. Praise the Lord that there is no necessary causal relationship between our behavior and our future, final destiny!

Otherwise, who can be saved? Who can get away from the Adam of the past and see the coming Christ? Only the gospel of grace reigning can lead to the type of worldview that acknowledges that even though someone may curse me out of evil motivations, he is still one of God's instruments for fulfilling the good work of the gospel. It ultimately leads to my justification, sanctification, and glorification. Maybe my disease, failure, and helplessness come from Satan's attacks, but even Satan can be sent or allowed by God.

This abundant, royal grace can be so great that all of the suffering, adversities, and helplessness in our lives are opportunities for grace to descend upon us. Because grace reigns, grace is not only the way God saves and forgives me; it is also the way God trains and reigns in me. Grace not only removes our sin, it also transforms our circumstances. When we are at the end of our rope, it grants us a death-exemption medal.

The reign of grace means that except for the grace of Christ, there is nothing substantial in my life because everything else in my life is for the purpose of leading me to his grace. Grace means that suffering and sin are no longer final. Except the death and resurrection of Jesus Christ, there is nothing in my life that has ultimate purpose. Grace reigning means refusing human independence and autonomy. Grace reigning means that we must seek righteousness outside ourselves.

Brothers and sisters, let us bravely admit we are beggars. Let us admit that we pastors and preachers are a group of useless servants. Let us admit that ever since we believed in the Lord, we daily offend our God in thought, word, and deed. Let us admit how good we are at rejecting and resisting grace while showing off our beauty, piety, gifts, and the fruit of our service. Let us admit that we are always afraid of people finding out how corrupt, impure, and full of failure we are. Let us admit that we always want people to know we piously love the Lord. Let us admit all of these together.

For the revival of Christ's church, for the spread of the gospel all over China, for the formation of more churches where grace reigns, for service in this dark age, let us seek the righteousness that is outside ourselves in the Lord Jesus Christ. Let us turn all of our wealth and our hope to the suffering servant, the king on the cross. He removed our sin, and he took away our chastisement. He makes grace the governing principle in our lives. Surely, he has borne our transgressions and was crushed for our iniquities.

*Lord, we praise you because you are the God who needs nothing; instead you poured yourself out and poured grace onto us. Lord, we pray that you would give us grace.*

*Lord, crush us so that we would know we are not beams but reeds; we are not fine gold but jars of clay. Lord, heal us so that we can grow in grace and be strengthened in grace. Lord, train us so that we can become doorkeepers for the key to heaven and boldly proclaim that the gospel of grace reigns in every city and every village in China. Lord, help us so that we can declare that sin and death no longer reign over this world.*

*Lord, may you use the mouths of these mortal men to open or shut the gates of heaven to lost souls.*

*Lord Jesus, let us say before you, "Lord Jesus, come!"*

## Reflect

- Wang Yi uses a famous Chinese poem to highlight the "ultimate concern" people feel in life. What things in your culture point to the "ultimate concern"?

- What is the difference between sin existing and sin reigning in your life?

- Reflect upon the statement, "Gratitude is now the only acceptable, legal motivation for sanctification." What does such gratitude look like in your life?

- Read Wang Yi's prayer. Take a moment before the Lord to admit you are a beggar and to "seek the righteousness that is outside" yourself.

# 2

# Being Devoured for the Glory of God

**Simon Liu**

*Simon Liu's conversion and calling to ministry came in one shot. When he said, "I want to be a Christian," for him it was the same as saying, "My whole life is for Christ now."*

*For many years, Liu was a successful businessman in Russia. He became a believer at an evangelistic meeting in the United States, after which he attended Reformed Theological  Seminary. He pastored and was involved in church planting for many years, and he is now committed to helping train and mentor new leaders. He also remains involved in ministry to the business world.*

> Their idols are silver and gold,
>     the work of human hands.
> They have mouths, but do not speak;
>     eyes, but do not see.
> They have ears, but do not hear;
>     noses, but do not smell.
> They have hands, but do not feel;
>     feet, but do not walk;
>     and they do not make a sound in their throat.
> Those who make them become like them;
>     so do all who trust in them.
>
> Psalm 115:4–8

One of my favorite writers in China is Shi Tiesheng. He is handicapped and uses a wheelchair, which has helped shape him into a great writer and thinker. He has summarized the human life in precisely three words: "loneliness, misery, and despair."

He says that whoever you are, if you live in this world and dare to think, you will find one thing to be sure—that life is doomed to be lonely. Whatever you think, however you want to approach others, and however close you are with someone, when you get up in the deep of the night, you will discover that you are a lonely person in this universe. Even with the closest person beside you, there is a sense of loneliness that you cannot avoid. Therefore, he says that life is doomed to be lonely. There is no way out.

Even worse, he says that life is doomed to be miserable. We pursue happiness throughout our lives, but he says we are doomed to misery because our abilities are limited but our desires are not. Yesterday you said that you would be happy to earn ten thousand RMB a year.[1] In the 1970s and 1980s, if you made ten thousand yuan, you were really something. Today in big cities like Beijing and Shanghai, most middle-class people have annual household incomes of ten thousand yuan, but they have become the "moonlight tribe."[2] When you have ten thousand, you dream of having a hundred thousand; when you have a hundred thousand, you dream of having a million; when you have a million, you dream of having ten million. Even if you became the richest man in the world, it would not change. Someone interviewed the richest man in the world, asking him, "What gives you satisfaction? Are you satisfied today?" He replied, "I would be satisfied if I could only have one more penny." Your ability will never catch up to your desire, so you are doomed to be miserable.

We experience loneliness, misery, and then finally despair, which is even more horrible. Once someone is born, we say he is alive, but from another perspective, the moment you are born, you are approaching death. When we say we are alive today, it can be expressed in another way—today we are dying. Humans have tried all kinds of ways to remove death from their memories and their lives.

1. About $1,500 US dollars. Renminbi (RMB) is the basic currency of China. Yuan is the more common term to refer to Chinese currency.

2. A colloquial term used for those who spend all of their income and save none.

But I am sorry to say that death does not wait; it will come, and no one can escape from it.

This is life you see. Whoever you are, even if you drive a BMW or Mercedes, you can never drive yourself to heaven. When you fly in an airplane, you may be a little closer to heaven, but it does not guarantee you can make it there. Your gold and silver, American dollars, RMB, and Hong Kong dollars cannot buy you a ticket to heaven. You cannot control another person's destiny. Even worse, you cannot control your own destiny.

Since mankind came to understand life as such, we have tried everything to find a solution. Since the fall of Adam and Eve, humans have been trying to figure out how to live this life. Through Psalm 115, God reveals in a few verses all that humans have been trying.

Idols are miserable. Augustine once said that idols are the most miserable; even dead men are better than the idols. Dead men at least lived for a while, but idols know nothing about life and death.

Strangely, those who make idols gradually become like them. When someone makes an idol, he thinks that he can gain control through it. But when you want to control others, you become controlled by Satan, and this is the scariest. There is a saying in China that goes, "Clever people fall victim to their own cleverness." You think you outsmart others, but the moment you deceive another, Satan has already slowly brought you into his net. Think about it. We Chinese believe we are the cleverest. No one else in the world is as smart as the Chinese. No one else is like us, going to all lengths to figure out all the loopholes. Yet we are relegated to being the hardest-working people. You think you are something, but once you start playing tricks, Satan has taken hold of you.

This passage tells us that if you worship an idol, you will become like it.

## A Society of False Gods

The world we live in is a world of false gods. In this passage, the idols are all visible, made by human hands. But today, these idols have been disguised in other forms that we do not often see in our lives. What is the most magnificent building in your city? If it is a financial tower or a bank, that shows the city's worship of wealth. If government offices take up the most magnificent buildings and cover the most area, it shows the city's worship of power. If the nightclubs and shopping malls are the most splendid, it shows people's worship of material comfort and lust. False worship is still with us today, and both in our past and present, we take part in making and worshiping false gods. We live entirely within our idols.

In China some people imagine, especially in our culture, that people can be perfect, but this is the biggest lie of all. When I was in elementary school, there were four portraits hanging in our classroom: Marx, Engels, Lenin, and Stalin, the four founders of communism. Later we found out these were four demons and four womanizers. Lenin was an activist for violence, a treacherous politician, and a client of prostitutes who died from a sexually transmitted disease. Recently, Russia declared that Lenin's body would be sent back to his hometown. They realized that Russians no longer liked Lenin. But since so many Chinese go to visit Lenin's tomb while in Russia, they decided to move Lenin's body to his hometown and let the Chinese tourists pay for it. The Chinese still think that maybe someone can be perfect. We are still hoping for a savior from China.

A while ago someone made an interesting summary of Chinese society online. He said that there were fifteen strange things happening in Chinese society.

First, the good Samaritan is blackmailed by the one he helps.

Second, people owe huge debts in order to buy houses and cars.

Third, middle school and grade school students are dating.

Fourth, there is a great race toward being neither man nor woman.

Fifth, communists and officials worship at temples.

Sixth, our single children are petulant.

Seventh, people vacation together in search of idleness.

Eighth, TV stations are filled with pharmaceutical ads.

Ninth, the powerful and rich are migrating to foreign countries.

Tenth, there is an increasing number of "dragon clocks."[3]

Eleventh, due to traffic congestion, biking is faster that driving.

Twelfth, political seats can be bought for a price.

Thirteenth, most officials are basically corrupt.

Fourteenth, rich people have more than one wife, as if there is no law.

Fifteenth, the waterways and skies are all polluted.

3. Colloquial for the aging population.

These are the consequences of idol worship, false god worship. The Bible tells us that when we start to worship false gods, we are enslaved by them. And a society of false gods is a dog-eat-dog society.

Since the fall, humans have been best at harming and devouring each other. If you try to understand the history of the entire world, you will see that the whole of human history since the fall is one of men harming and devouring each other. Today, your nation has ravaged this nation; tomorrow, that nation will in turn consume yours. Even so-called eras of peace are merely times when people ingested each other more gracefully.

Sometimes, they feed on you so skillfully that you do not even feel like you are being eaten up. Sometimes they gobble you jokingly. Sometimes they have to feed on you ethically; sometimes they feed on you legally. Sometimes they devour you with violence. Sometimes they ingest you with limits; sometimes they absorb you without limit. When you strive for your own interests while ignoring the interests of others, you are devouring the people around you. You live only for your own benefit, preparing to devour others.

Therefore, we find our society to be one in which people trick each other, hurt each other, hate each other, curse each other, envy each other, dislike each other, and devour each other. This is the consequence of idol worship.

But thanks be to the Lord! God reveals this to us, saying that the worship of false gods is nothing more than humans devouring each other. Humans have attempted all manner of graceful ways of devouring others. But God says, "No, as long as you worship false gods, you are devouring others." He knows that even if you want to be good and say that you will not devour others, you cannot do it. God reveals this to us and shows us the reality of human nature and the true image of society. But let us understand that the Lord is not only the God who reveals; he is also the God who saves.

Psalm 115:9–15 reveals two crucial, corresponding topics: trusting and blessing. There is a Chinese idiom 三番四次, which means "over and over again." When you hear someone telling you something over and over again, it means he is serious about it. When God tells you something over and over, God is serious about it. God emphasizes trust three times and blessing four times to show how much he wants to bless you. He says, "Trust me, and you will be blessed."

The purpose of salvation is for humanity to be blessed by the loving God; therefore, we see from the Old Testament that God keeps demonstrating his willingness to bless men. We see God call Abraham, "Abraham, come out." Abraham trusted God, and God blessed him and made him the father of many nations. And God kept calling people and blessing those who trusted him. Even when the gentile prostitute was willing to trust him, he blessed her. Our God is one who blesses.

But relying on obedience does not guarantee being blessed. Human nature is such that I will obey depending on how much you will bless me. Human obedience is inherently selfish. You want my obedience? Fine. How much are you going to give me? Whenever God said, "I will make you the father of many nations," Abraham probably thought it was a good deal since he had no children, and it wouldn't hurt to give it a try. After all, he had nothing to lose. The Chinese say, "It is better to believe than not to believe." Such obedience is selfish. When we start to understand the Bible, we find that all such obedience is just a reflection pointing to the ultimate obedience: the complete obedience of the Son of God.

We see that Jesus Christ came into this world with all authority, but out of his own initiative, he gave up everything and came into this world with nothing. He said that he was willing to obey, and he obeyed so that sinners could be blessed. This is true obedience. When your obedience is for your own blessing, it is not true obedience. It is just your ability to be smart enough to make a deal. Therefore, we see that the obedience of Jesus Christ guarantees the transfer of all grace and blessing to Jesus.

When we believe in him, we say that we believe we are in Christ. Our blessed assurance is not that I keep a certain distance from him. My blessed assurance is that I must fully enter Jesus Christ. From history we see that all who have believed in Jesus Christ have understood this point— Jesus's obedience leads to my blessing, and my obedience can lead to blessing many others.

## The Blessings and Temptations of the Church

What is the church? The church is our obedience, which leads to blessing the world. Today many of us come to the church, saying, "If I am obedient, then I am blessed." This is wrong; it is still idol worship. The church is the manifestation of our obedience to God, which brings blessing to others. Therefore, we see Paul, Peter, and others in the apostolic age being obedient and bringing blessings to other regions. Missions began, and the church came into existence.

Let us think about how the Chinese have been blessed. Every one of us who sits here today is blessed because other Christians were obedient. If there was no Christianity, there would be no modern civilization of China. On July 4, 1949, the former vice chairman of the Communist Party, Liu Shaoqi, wrote to Stalin that British and American churches had built thirty-one colleges, twenty-nine libraries, and 320 middle and primary schools in China. Think about how much the British and American churches alone did for China.

Additionally, I believe all Chinese women should be grateful to the Lord God. Had God not sent missionaries to China, your feet might still be bound.[4] Had missionaries not opened women's schools, Chinese women might not have the right to education today.

---

4. Foot binding was a widespread custom originating in the tenth century wherein the feet of women were bound at a young age, deforming the bone structure and severely limiting mobility. The practice was considered a symbol of status and beauty. It was finally eradicated in the twentieth century.

Chinese children should be grateful to the Lord God. Today we say there are 1.5 billion people in China, a nation with a huge population. Missionaries brought advanced delivery methods to China when the infant mortality rate was about 50 percent, without which the Chinese population could by no means have reached what it is today.

Disabled people in China should be grateful to God because missionaries opened the earliest schools and hospitals for the disabled in China.

Chinese men should be grateful to God because the Lord God granted us real modern education and saved our mothers and daughters.

And on a lighter note, many of us love peanuts from Shandong and apples from Yantai city. Both of these were brought by missionaries, and we all know that they are delicious!

God took care of our women and children, and how did we treat God's bride, his church? In the Boxer Rebellion in 1900, 241 foreign missionaries were killed. Forty percent of them were women, and 20 percent of them were children. In other words, when our heroic Boxers, a big group of men, wielded their swords toward the missionaries, over 60 percent of them were unarmed women and children. God sent his servants to take care of our women and children, and our men killed their women and children.

When I think about all of this, I feel that we Chinese must repent of our debts. We have never thanked God for our mothers and sisters who can walk and run. We do not say, "My mother and my sisters, you don't have to walk with your feet bound. You can come out and have a job." You hated God's church, but the Lord kept sending his servants to save this land. Because of his obedience, Christ delivers salvation so that those who believe in him have the blessing of the heavenly kingdom.

We bit the hand that fed us. But God says, "I give blessings upon blessings."

The Chinese love to eat, and we often say that we eat everything with four legs except for benches; we eat anything with two legs except for humans. But everyone who lives in this world has devoured the Son of God. We killed the Son of God, and the amazing thing is, God actually allows us to feed on him.

Let us read Psalm 115:16–18. Trusting we are blessed, trusting in Christ who allows us to receive all blessing in himself, God reveals:

> The heavens are the Lord's heavens,
> but the earth he has given to the children of man.
> The dead do not praise the Lord,
> nor do any who go down into silence.
> But we will bless the Lord
> from this time forth and forevermore.
> Praise the Lord!

Under the marvelous preservation of the Spirit, this gospel has been proclaimed through the generations until it reached us. We are blessed. The Chinese church today has indeed been through a lot of brilliant development. Our numbers have increased; our knowledge has increased; our evangelism and testimonies have increased. Glory be to God! But eating habits die hard in Chinese culture. When people from this dog-eat-dog society begin to believe in God, will they continue in the same strange behavior of this society, where people devour each other?

There is a horrible phenomenon of devouring the church today. When people from a dog-eat-dog society come into the church, their old habits die hard. When people do not truly understand the gospel, they keep their cannibalistic nature.

First, I will emphasize the problem of pastors devouring the church. People become pastors or ministers and they impose their leadership style. Pastoral training can be like Communist Party school training. Mission trips become traveling at the church's expense; reception of visiting pastors turns into fine dining at the church's expense. Pastors spend more time in meetings than in prayer, and more time soaking in scenery than in preaching. Ordination becomes job access on the route from internships to full-time employment. Church schools turn into schools for the children of ministers. Ministers become allies; seminaries become the training grounds of denominations. Church planting becomes the work of the planter alone; stewards become owners, and servants become masters. They claim to be willing martyrs for the Lord but often travel abroad to escape from the smog with their families; when they are abroad, they travel to churches to collect support on behalf of the pastors who are actually on the front line.

And in the end, the name of God becomes the name of the people. These are the unhealthy phenomena I have seen.

But we are family members, and we must name these things and point them out clearly. Some of us often feel that we are at a disadvantage for serving the Lord. People often ask me, "You were doing business and making good money; why then would you become a poor preacher?"

When my father heard about my decision, he asked me how I would support my wife and children. I said I would rely on God. He said, "Stop this nonsense! You should rely on someone else." Let me tell you, even if you do not serve Jesus Christ, you cannot guarantee you will become a billionaire. And do not think that because I serve God, therefore I must be poor. In fact, we just made the most cost-effective deal. We must not think that we are heroic in serving God; after all, we do not work daily under the fire of submachine guns. We still live ordinary lives. Many of our pains are not even as severe as the pains of the world. After all, we have the best boss in heaven.

The space of our public worship is increasing, and because of it, house church pastors are facing great temptations as well as confusions of identity. At this moment, we must pay special attention to the temptation of Satan and the guidance of the Holy Spirit. We know some people are always calculating ways to go from being an ordinary house church pastor to a large church pastor, from a pastor of one church to a leader of several churches, from a pastor in one city to a pastor of national or even international fame.

Someone once said jokingly that even the Lord Jesus had only twelve disciples, one of which was a failure; so, you shouldn't think too much of yourself. Pastoring a church is very hard. I have exhausted all of my abilities and am still left with a few dozen people, most of whose salvation I have no confidence in.

But praise the Lord! God says, "You must trust in me, for Jesus Christ is the only way, the truth, and the life." You repeatedly talk about trusting in your pastor, but if you trust him long enough and become familiar with him, you will find him increasingly not so trustworthy, which is normal. Brothers and sisters, if your pastor does not weep for the believers in your church, you should weep for your pastor. If your pastor sheds no tears, you should be warned and weep for him, so that he might shed tears for you. We come with the Lord's commission to take care of his children, yet we come from a dog-eat-dog society with all of our old habits; and we have to look after those who are even more prone to devouring others. We face great conflict and great difficulties, and we desperately need prayer.

Let us look at the problem of believers devouring the church. Another feature of the Chinese character is disobedience and unruliness, which is reflected in the church.

The Reformation brought down the universal authority of the pope and brought the separation of powers in the West; but when it came to China, it made every one of us the pope. The attitude has become, "So what if you are a pastor? Don't we believe in the priesthood of all believers?"

Relationships among the Chinese are centered on personal interests. A pastor once said that believers in the Chinese church are like locusts—they swarm into a church that has resources, consume them, and then, upon locating another church with resources, they go to swarm into that church. These people fly to and fro and devour every church they go to.

Not only so, but the church also has a serious problem teaching its second generation. We enjoy critiquing the problems of the second generation of the rich and the elite children of government officials. But we as Christian parents still face great challenges, and we still hold high hopes for our offspring. We long for our children to succeed in life, and they have become our idols. When you say you are Christian but worship your children as idols, the first ones to see through you will be your children. They will say, "Our parents are hypocrites."

Many Christians today are like this. We observe a dog-eat-dog society; the church is devoured by its own, and many Christians are astonished all day long. We complain that our pastor is like this, our church is like that, and society is like so. We are astonished by how fast housing prices are soaring. We are shocked at the high cost of children's education and how unethical public school teachers are becoming. We see doctors without medical ethics; we are stunned by food fraud. We are shocked by the corruption, crimes, and promiscuity of famous pastors; our brothers and sisters' love of the world; the division of the church by our elders and pastors; and the lack of spiritual maturity.

We are constantly in a state of being surprised. When we are in the world, we realize that the world is horrifying. But when we come into the church and stay there long enough, we find it horrifying as well.

Dear brothers and sisters, today we see society overheating. The temperature is rising, and the church is also overheating. Do not forget that God does not plan for us to be thermometers but rather people of a fixed temperature. Do not be transformed by the changes in the world, but transform the world.

Therefore, Psalm 115:16–17 says, "The heavens are the Lord's heavens, but the earth he has given to the children of man. The dead do not praise the Lord, nor do any who go down into silence."

God is not competing for space with men, saying, "I cannot rule over this; it's yours." On the contrary, God is saying, "You cannot come up to the heaven and rule over it, so I entrust the earth to you, and you shall rule over it."

Since the creation, humans have been entrusted with the ability and duty to rule over the earth, but we have failed and been unable to do so.

## Feeding on Christ

So how can we rule over the earth? How can we solve its issues? God gives us a very simple method. Please remember it.

It is, "To be eaten."

## Being Devoured for the Glory of God

We say this is a dog-eat-dog world, and yet we are surprised when people devour the church. God says, "Let's change it up, and I will make you to be devoured." God calls us through Paul's words in Romans 12:1: "I appeal to you therefore, brothers, by the mercies of God, to present your bodies as a living sacrifice, holy and acceptable to God, which is your spiritual worship." This does not mean you are to be put on an altar, for there is no altar anymore. Rather, God says that to offer your body means you are going to be eaten. In a dog-eat-dog society, you will learn and practice how to be eaten. For all Christians, pastors or lay believers, offering your body to God means offering yourself to the church and practicing being devoured.

As pastors, we might have a member come and say to us, "Pastor, your sermon today was awful. Couldn't you spend more time preparing it?" Many of us might respond by praying, "Lord, chase this member out of here. Take him away!" But God says, "No, even if he leaves, I will send ten more your way." Dear pastors, have you found that in your church, there are always a few people who are against you? God says you should practice being devoured.

To love others means suffering. Love leads to pain. Brothers and sisters should practice responding to sin, allowing themselves to experience what it is like to be devoured. As God says, "In the church of the Lord, you should have love for one another and forgive each other. This is what must be implemented in my kingdom. You are safe in the church, because this is my house. I have clearly instructed you to learn how to love one another; that is, to be devoured by others."

Today he bites you, and it hurts! Tomorrow you bite him, and it hurts! And then we say, "Praise the Lord," because it is nothing compared to the pain of the cross. This ought to be practiced in the church. Then, after enough practice in the church and having developed Christ-like stature, you will be sent into this dog-eat-dog society to be devoured.

In the story of Jesus feeding five thousand people with five loaves and two fish in Luke 9, the disciples say they don't have enough food for the five thousand people with them. Jesus says, "You give them something to eat." This passage demonstrates that when you are well practiced in the church, you are ready to go out into the world. To be devoured by this world means to genuinely suffer, to be taken advantage of, to sacrifice; then, in that moment, the world will begin to change.

Today the Chinese church has much to learn from visiting places all over the world and observing churches that are big, churches famous for church governance, and churches well known for discipleship. But the starting point is learning to be devoured. Among the savviest groups of people, getting the short end of the stick is the biggest blessing the living God gives you. If you want to compete against the people of the world to see who is more ruthless, you will be miserable. Therefore, we see that we have to lay aside our conceit and identify ourselves with the cross.

Martin Luther once said, "Now it is not sufficient for anyone, and it does him no good to recognize God in his glory and majesty, unless he recognizes him in the humility and shame of the cross." You can claim to glorify God, but you will give up once someone takes advantage of you, and that does no good to anyone. John Calvin also said, "We never truly glory in him until we have utterly discarded our own glory." In a world where everyone wants to take advantage of others, we glorify God by seeking to be taken advantage of. In a world where everyone seeks pleasure, we glorify God by seeking to suffer and give of ourselves. In a corrupt, dog-eat-dog society, we give ourselves to be devoured by others.

In a world where everyone is doomed to die, we become vessels of the life-giving Jesus Christ, who gives away the bread of life. The Chinese often greet one another with, "Have you eaten?" Brothers and sisters, next time someone greets you this way, you should remind them, "I don't eat people. I want you to feed on me."

This can only be done by returning to the most fundamental point—feeding on the Lord. Without feeding on the Lord, you cannot face this world. The Lord Jesus says, "My flesh is true food, and my blood is true drink." He also says, "Unless you eat the flesh of the Son of Man and drink his blood, you have no life in you" (John 6:55, 53).

As Chinese Christians, we have this special characteristic of living in a culture full of pleasantries where we always say, "No thanks, I won't be eating." Without feeding on Jesus, you will not realize how much he loves you. Without feeding on him, you will not understand his sacrificial love. Once you do understand, you will find that you must first feed on the Lord so that others can feed on you. The more I feed on the Lord, the happier I am when others feed on me. When

When the Spirit of the Lord is with me, my spirit is with the Lord.

When you drink the blood of Christ, you have in yourself Christ's DNA. Your DNA bears the DNA of the cross, and you become salt and light to this world. We glorify God because he is the God of revelation; he reveals to us who the true God is and who the false gods are. False gods are horrible in their feeding on men. To God be the glory, for he is the God who saves. He knew we couldn't save ourselves, so he came to save us. He first makes us feed on him and taste the sweetness of the Lord's grace, and then he prepares us to be a blessing for the world through being devoured. Because he gave unto us, we are able to give in return. To God be the glory, for he is the God who cares and supplies. The more we are willing to bless this world, the more God is willing to bless us. And God especially helps us to realize that if we become obedient only for our own blessing, then this is a self-centered faith. We become obedient so that others may be blessed. This is true faith that brings glory to God; this is true faith in Christ.

So finally, let us return to Psalm 115:1, which says, "Not to us, O Lord, not to us, but to your name give glory, for the sake of your steadfast love and your faithfulness!" As I said, all will die. Where will you be after death? Every description of the angels and the heavenly host depicts them praising, worshiping, and falling down on the ground. In the new heavens and new earth, there is no famous pastor, no investiture of the gods, no individual glory; instead all glory is attributed to the Lamb. All your pursuits for your own sake have nothing to do with heaven. If you are going to heaven for your own sake, you are not destined for heaven. Therefore, from today—this moment, this era—we must practice true worship.

In the context of Chinese culture, we must learn how to glorify God by being devoured.

Lord, our God and our king, we are here today to exalt you.

Our mouths turn to you today. We are a group of people who need true repentance. Daily we praise you and say we will love you forever. Yet when we come out of this world, we bear with us all sorts of things, and feeding on others is merely one of them. Lord, we come before your throne of grace. Help us, show mercy to us.

When we say we praise you daily and forever, may it be your will that we offer our bodies as living sacrifices and become a group of people who are pleasing to you, redeemed by you, cleansed by the precious blood of Jesus Christ, and feeding on Jesus Christ forever. Because great is the Lord, and you are greatly to be praised. Our generation shall tell the coming generation of your mighty deeds that transform us in this dog-eat-dog society.

We shall proclaim your power that transforms us from being villains, womanizers, those who love the world, and those who love our own reputations. Lord, as we meditate on your glorious splendor and your wondrous works, let us speak of your mighty and awesome name and declare your greatness. You sent your Son into this world. Prompt us to say, "Lord, your grace cannot be hidden within us. We shall sing praise for your righteousness."

As the psalmist says, "The Lord is gracious and merciful." You are "slow to anger" and will not open the earth to swallow us. You are good to all; your grace is shown to all of us. Lord, we love because you first loved us.

As we stand in awe before you, willing to be devoured by others, Lord, give us power and courage to say, "Lord, unite us with Jesus Christ who was devoured by sin and death on the cross." Today, you have made him the highest, leading us to realize the truth and become your holy people. We will declare the glory of your kingdom, speak of your power of transformation, and make known to our dog-eat-dog society your power and the majesty of your kingdom, because your kingdom and your dominion endure forever and ever.

When we say we are to be devoured, it means that like the Lord, we will uphold all who are falling and raise up all who are bowed down. When people or livestock ask for food, the Lord opens his hands and gives food to them, satisfying the desire of every living thing. We are willing to suffer with your Son in your abundant grace, full of your steadfast love and faithfulness, as you are the one who is faithful. Lord, you are near to us; you help us because your protection exceeds the harm that others bring to us — their bites and devouring of us. But one day, you will destroy all the wicked and save those of us who are standing from the final judgment.

Our mouths and hearts will speak the praises of the Lord. Anoint those who stand in awe before you with the Spirit of the Lord so that today we can see Jesus Christ on the cross; Jesus Christ who ascended to heaven with glory and honor. He rose again from the dead and grants us the power of eternity that cannot be devoured by this world. Protect us as we enter into the midst of wolves, into this world, as we know you are with us. Bless the men and women who stand in awe before you, as we do not trust our own power to cover ourselves.

Lord, we thank you! You sent many missionaries to us who were devoured in China in the past centuries; today they bear great witness to us. They weep for our indifference and lack of *understanding of your will and your plan for your kingdom; they weep for church growth. We stand in awe before you, knowing that we cannot be transformed in one day. But we believe that your power will descend on us so that we are willing to be devoured by others, because life must be shaped by you in such suffering.*

*Thank you, gracious Lord, for being with us so that as we join together to run the road to heaven, we will learn how not to argue with one another and not to bite each other. For God says that when we bite each other in such a way, the church will be devoured. Lord, come help us to see our evil so that when we repent before you, we may see the beauty of the Lord. You loved us to the point of letting your Son die; it is us who bit and devoured him. Lord, help us to see, so that when we suffer, we do not trust in ourselves but are in union with the risen Jesus Christ. When we are united with him, such devouring is transformed into suffering with a willing heart. Hear our prayer, and bless those of us who are willing to be living sacrifices.*

*You are with us because your divine power covers us, because the power of the resurrection is in us. Even if we are persecuted by the sword and distress is around us, when we are struck down, we will stand up again. We have this treasure in jars of clay, and it cannot be changed. Lord, protect us. Hear our prayers as we entrust them to what is totally trustworthy—not trusting in idols, but trusting in the power of the true God, so that they will never be devoured from their eternal calling.*

*Hear our prayer, Lord.*

*We pray in the name of our Lord Jesus Christ. Amen!*

## Reflect

- Simon Liu says, "When you strive for your own interests while ignoring the interests of others, you are devouring the people around you." Can you give an example of this from life?

- How can you practice being devoured in your church in order to prepare for going into the world?

- Simon Liu argues that the only way to stop devouring others is to be devoured yourself; he also argues that we can only have the ability to be devoured if we first feed on Christ. In what ways do you regularly feed on Christ?

# 3

# Faith: The Sole Connection between God and Man

## Peng Qiang

Peng Qiang went to a prestigious college started by the Communist Party to prepare its next generation of leaders, but instead of becoming a Party leader, he submitted to Christ. Afterward, he started a Christian publishing house in Chengdu. After publishing books for many years, he studied at International Theological Seminary in the United States and entered the pastorate in China.

Peng Qiang has spent much of his career studying church history and creating new, creative, thoughtful resources for the church in China. His influence in China is wide due to the lectures he gives in churches across the country.

Now faith is the assurance of things hoped for, the conviction of things not seen. For by it the people of old received their commendation. By faith we understand that the universe was created by the word of God, so that what is seen was not made out of things that are visible.

By faith Abel offered to God a more acceptable sacrifice than Cain, through which he was commended as righteous, God commending him by accepting his gifts. And through his faith, though he died, he still speaks. By faith Enoch was taken up so that he should not see death, and he was not found, because God had taken him. Now before he was taken he was commended as having pleased God. And without faith it is impossible to please him, for whoever would draw near to God must believe that he exists and that he rewards those who seek him. By faith Noah, being warned by God concerning events as yet unseen, in reverent fear constructed an ark for the saving of his household. By this he condemned the world and became an heir of the righteousness that comes by faith.

Hebrews 11:1–7

A contemporary sociologist of religion, Peter Berger, invented an insightful term: "a world without windows." He says people of the modern age live without a window to the transcendent, existing instead according to their basic senses, what they can see and touch. He is describing modern people who have lost the ability to see through faith. They have lost hope in a world that is unseen, and their souls and hearts are poor.

What Berger describes is in contrast to people of a classical Christian worldview who live in a world with windows. For example, today I might be sick or encounter an economic crisis, or my family might face a variety of challenges. For someone who lives in a world with windows, he still has hope. He still knows that outside the window, there is a blue sky. But people of the modern age are wretched because they live in a world without windows. Therefore, the power you see is power; the bondage of wealth you see is bondage; the afflictions you see are afflictions. People of the modern age do not live in a realm that depends on faith; they live by what they see. All you see today is all you have, and this is a desperate condition.

People who do not start from faith usually pursue their own values in various ways. Some base their lives on the need for self-actualization; some base their lives on their preferences; and some rely on trends and define themselves by what is popular today. In a word, the desires of the flesh, the desires of the eyes, and the pride of this life all reflect a typical lifestyle based on what the eyes can see and on personal interests. But from God's perspective, whatever does not proceed from faith is sin.

Hebrews 11:6 says, "Without faith it is impossible to please him." Our life will not be acceptable to God if the values of our lives do not start from belief in God. How we live, how we offer up our life, how we set up our schedule—we cannot live a life by sight and not by faith. Life by faith is the only legitimate condition in the relationship between God and man.

## The Critical Nature of Faith

In Paul's words, the Christian faith is not by works of the law but by faith. Our passage in Hebrews says, "Without faith it is impossible to please God." If you look at the examples of Abel and Enoch, you will see clearly why this truth is critical.

In Genesis 4, Abel brought the firstborn and their fat portions from his flock to the Lord, while Cain brought an offering of the fruit of the ground. Genesis 4 says specifically that the Lord had regard for Abel and his offering, but for Cain and his offering he had no regard. This does not mean that God eats meat but does not eat vegetables; rather, God had regard for this person and for his heart, so he accepted his offering. Genesis says that God simply accepted Abel. Hebrews further explains that God did this because of his faith; consequently, because Abel had faith that God had accepted him, he willingly offered his best. When Abel was killed by Cain, it was a tragedy according to the world's standard. But Hebrews says he was accepted by God, and though he died, he still speaks to us today through his faith.

This passage also discusses another person, Enoch. He walked with God for three hundred years. Many people envy Enoch and say, "If only I were like Enoch, I could be taken up so that I would not see death." We Chinese may easily confuse Enoch with the gods who hide in the mountains, floating around for several years and then suddenly disappearing. But if you read the genealogy in Genesis closely, you will discover who Enoch encountered in his lifetime. Enoch lived in the generation of Lamech, who, like Cain, was notorious for his violence. Enoch did not live in a utopia like a god; rather, he held onto and depended on God through faith in an evil age. As such, Hebrews says God accepted him and commends him for pleasing God.

So we have two examples, Abel and Enoch. By worldly standards, they seemed to have two different destinies: one was murdered, while the other did not taste death and was taken up by God. It seems that through this contrast, the author wanted to tell us not to look at their worldly destinies to determine their status before God. They were accepted by God through their faith. Faith opened the eyes of Abel and Enoch to see God and see the value of life. They understood what it meant to offer the best to God and that the purpose of life was to walk with God. God accepted their faith and commended them for pleasing him.

Why is faith important? Because in faith lies the sole legitimate relationship between God and man—man gives glory to God as instructed by him, and we come to him just as we are. Faith gives the children of God eyes to see that everything comes from his grace. Faith links all that we have today with God's grace. Faith teaches us that all things are from him and through him and for him, and to him be all glory.

## Faith as a Connection

This truth is still relevant for us today. Every morning when I leave home, I pass by a hotpot restaurant. The manager requires all the staff members in the restaurant to call out slogans to start the day. The last slogan is always, "Do you all have faith today [in a booming business]?" And all repeatedly shout back, "Yes we do!"

Hebrews 11:1 says, "Faith is the assurance of things hoped for, the conviction of things not seen." Have you seen the things you hope for? You have not. Have you taken hold of the things you hope for? You have not. Yet, you have assurance through faith for the things you hope for. You already have a guarantee today. The assurance of things hoped for means that you have already grasped the remote things that have been destined for you as if you had already taken hold of them.

The conviction of things not seen means that faith enables us to be certain about a world that we cannot see. Augustine says that faith makes us confident about the invisible world. Calvin says it even more beautifully, "Faith puts the invisible worlds on display." By faith the invisible world is on display for you today.

Faith brings assurance in that future hope. Faith not only gives us firm belief in the invisible world, it puts it on display. Therefore, we can see that the two characteristics of faith in Hebrews share one thing in common: faith as a connector. Faith connects the visible to the invisible; the things of today to the things of the future; the limited to the unlimited. For someone who lives by faith, it connects a sinner who has received grace to the holy God. Faith is not just a concept. It is a connection.

Often people say, "Brother Zhang has a large faith," as if they were saying that this person has a faith that weighs eight ounces, and that person has a faith that weighs two. But faith is a condition, a connection. Who you connect to by faith determines what kind of worldview you live within. That connection puts your worldview on display. Faith in the gospel means that you are connected with the kingdom of God and the King of the kingdom, and you live within a gospel worldview.

Hebrews puts on display a gospel worldview manifested by faith. Verse 3 says, "By faith we understand that the universe was created by the word of God, so that what is seen was not made out of things that are visible." By faith we understand the origin of the whole universe, that it was created by the Word of God. This visible world was made out of nothing. It is a declaration of a Christian worldview, that the universe was created by God's Word and made from nothing. It is by faith that we embrace this spiritual knowledge and revelation.

This verse also mentions "by faith we." "We" represents Christians at the time of writing, the saints throughout the ages, and believers today, including all of us. Through God's revelation in the prophets and the apostles, by faith we understand a gospel worldview, who God is, human nature, how man can be saved in Christ, and the world's hope for the future. Because we believe, therefore we know.

Faith: The Sole Connection between God and Man

As we believe, we continue to seek deeper understanding of ourselves and of God. Christian epistemology says, "I believe, therefore I know; I believe, therefore I understand." Therefore, knowledge and understanding of the gospel worldview is not from reason to reason. It originates from our faith and goes from faith to faith.

That is why the Bible says, "The fear of the Lord is the beginning of wisdom." Without a faith based on truth, one falls into either atheism or agnosticism, as if controlled by some unknowable, invisible power. Without faith, one's understanding and knowledge of the world will be broken.

You can imagine this mountain could be controlled by a mountain god, or this sea could be controlled by an ocean god. Such a broken understanding would never lead to science. Without faith, our understanding of life is also broken. We will be like individual atoms, each searching for his own purpose and doing what is right in his own eyes, but never quite locating ourselves.

But the worldview embedded in the gospel of creation and salvation leads us to clearly understand that our purpose is given by the Creator and Savior. The author is not talking about abstract ideas here. These Hebrew believers were facing persecution. They were tempted to give up their faith in Christ and go back to the old ways. Here the author is actually reminding this group of people that the foundation of this world is God and his unchanging Word. Therefore, do not be influenced by your feelings or the momentary afflictions that surround you today. The author reminds his readers that beyond this visible world there is an invisible world. And our purpose is connected to that invisible world.

As Paul says in 2 Corinthians 4:18, "We look not to the things that are seen but to the things that are unseen. For the things that are seen are transient, but the things that are unseen are eternal." This visible world connects to the invisible world through God's revelation, as God actively intervenes in human history through it. Through the Bible we come to understand the creation of the world. The climax of God's revelation is his son, Jesus Christ. God's son, Jesus Christ, is the evidence of this invisible world's strong interaction with the visible world. Jesus Christ is the manifestation of the invisible God and the invisible kingdom of God. The whole book of Hebrews is about the real object of faith, Jesus Christ.

The author goes to great lengths to prove that Jesus Christ is greater than Moses; he is greater than the angels and the chief priest of the Aaronic system. His obedience is the fountain of our salvation; his death and blood become the sacrifice of redemption once and for all. He is raised back to life and seated at the right hand of the Father, demonstrating that he has fulfilled the kingdom of God. Today he still reigns through his intercession and the promise of the gospel. Therefore, when the author talks about a gospel worldview here, he is not talking about abstract philosophy. He is teaching a basic truth about life and death. Through Christ Jesus we can come to know an invisible kingdom that is more real than the visible persecution of today, more real than the visible GDP, more real than concrete buildings, and more real than all visible power and wealth.

When we are captivated by the truth of the kingdom, attracted by its vision, and filled by its grace, that invisible kingdom will turn around and come inside us, motivating us and granting us power and grace.

Therefore, when we talk about faith, we are not talking about faith as some type of merit. The Holy Spirit enlightens us through the Bible and leads us back to a gospel worldview. This gospel worldview does not originate from our brain but from the revelation of the Holy Spirit. The Holy Spirit enables us to believe in the words of the Bible and its teachings about the kingdom of God. By faith we come into this kingdom. By faith we believe in Christ, the king of this kingdom, and accept this gospel worldview.

When we talk about "by faith alone," we are going back to the gospel worldview. Through the lens of faith, we begin to put back together all of the fragmented pieces of life, thought, and the world. We meditate on God's Word by faith, which is the revelation of the Bible.

The impact of that invisible world becomes more and more evident, to a point that not only our brains but also our souls can feel it. The invisible is more real than the visible. The baby in the manger is more comforting than all power. The love on the cross is sweeter than all the glory of the world. What is inside of us is bigger than even the world.

The significance of faith is not that I must take hold of certain merits that I did not have before. No. The Holy

Spirit opens our eyes and grants us faith. He brings us back into a gospel worldview, through which we see the invisible kingdom of God. Today that kingdom expands among us through the gospel of God's son, Jesus Christ. We see that the kingdom impacts the past, the present, and the future. It affects our identity and position in this kingdom, so we live out this worldview and respond to it by faith.

## The Heart of a Beggar

Let us read verse 6 again to understand what it would look like for someone to actually live by faith alone: "And without faith it is impossible to please him, for whoever would draw near to God must believe that he exists and that he rewards those who seek him." The one who draws near to God is the one living by faith. He has the dependent heart of a beggar, the trusting heart of a child, and the obedient and submissive heart of a servant.

Verse 6 mentions "whoever would draw near to God," but the Chinese translation does not convey the full meaning of "whoever." A more accurate translation would be "the person who draws near to God," or the person who takes shelter in God. It is not just a nodding acquaintance with God. It is to seek shelter, to depend on, to draw near. In plain language, it is saying that I have nothing, and as such, I give my life to you.

Please notice here that for a person to draw near to God and take shelter in him, that person must believe in the existence of God. Today, what it means to believe in God's existence has been treated casually in our contemporary language. "Oh, I believe there is a conference in Hong Kong right now." "Oh, I believe there may be some people among us sent to watch us closely." When we describe belief like this, it is way too frivolous. But when Hebrews talks about a person who seeks shelter in God—a person who draws near to God, offering everything he has, including his life—such a person must believe in the existence of God. Every moment of your life is in his presence. Your whole life is responsible to him, and you must give an account of your life to him.

If you honestly understood the significance of this belief, you would not stop shivering from fear. When you recognize God's existence, it actually feels dreadful. We are disobedient sinners. We often have our own schemes. Therefore, you come to understand why large portions of the previous chapters in Hebrews testify that without the grace of Christ, without Christ as our chief priest, and without Christ and the best sacrifice he offered, no one can stand firm. Without Christ, we cannot put on the robe of righteousness. Without Christ, we cannot draw near to the king of heaven.

This is the first condition of living in faith—the heart of a beggar seeking shelter. Living in faith demands the heart of a broken person, the heart of one who admits he is a sinner who seeks shelter in God. After all, only those with the hearts of children will really believe that he rewards those who seek him.

So far, the author of Hebrews has clearly helped the reader realize that God gives us assurance through the resurrected Christ and that in Christ, he accepts those who seek him. You know that the core of the Christian faith is the gospel. It is not just knowing God but also knowing what kind of God our God is. Our God is a good God. Without the heart of a child transformed by the gospel, without the Holy Spirit working inside us, we can never accept or believe the revelation of the gospel worldview that God not only exists but that he is also good.

You know this knowledge does not come from human observation. It can only come through the revelation of the gospel. When you see all the suffering in the world, when you see evil prosper, when you see good people suffer, when you suffer from serious illness yourself, when you would rather die than live, or when you face intense persecution like the author of Hebrews, will you still believe in the goodness of God?

When you face these adversities, you will either doubt God's existence, or you will conclude that even if he exists, he must be an eccentric old man who hates people and loves to make them suffer. We struggle to believe in both God's sovereignty and goodness. This trust is fundamentally grounded in the gospel of the Son of God: the death and resurrection of Jesus.

Elie Wiesel was a famous twentieth-century writer. He was Jewish, and he won the Nobel Peace Prize. I had always wondered why he won the prize for peace instead of the prize in literature. It is because he was a Holocaust survivor from Auschwitz.

# Faith: The Sole Connection between God and Man

His most famous work is *Night.* It is his autobiography as a concentration camp survivor, which retells the story of how he survived Auschwitz. He grew up in a very orthodox Jewish family. He read the Old Testament with a rabbi as a child. Whenever he read the Scriptures, he read with holiness. He said that it was the holy Word of God, and he felt drawn to God every time he read it. Yet in Auschwitz, his whole belief in God collapsed.

There were two critical incidents. The first happened just after he arrived at Auschwitz. He told his father, "We will never separate from each other, and I will never leave you." The next day, his father was whipped by a camp guard. His initial response was, "How could my father be whipped?" Then out of a desire to protect himself, he found himself asking, "What's wrong with my father?" He gradually realized his fury was no longer directed toward the guard but at his father. He was furious that his father did not know how to stay away from that evil guard. Afterward he was upset by his own indifference and how he could he treat his father like this in his heart. Then he described a young man who was also in the concentration camp with him. That young man was very pious. He loved to help others and had the face of an angel, but later he was brutally murdered.

In the past few decades, people have wondered how mankind can continue to write poems after Auschwitz. Similarly, people have asked how people can continue to believe in God after Auschwitz. For a long time, Wiesel could not get rid of his guilt as a survivor.

Interestingly enough, the friend who introduced the manuscript for *Night* to a French publisher was the French writer François Mauriac, who was a Christian. Mauriac wrote the afterword to the book, in which he expressed deep regret for not being able to comfort this Auschwitz survivor. How could he tell him that there is a God? How could he tell him that this God not only exists but also that he is good? Mauriac wrote in his afterword, "What did I say to him? Did I speak of that other Jew, his brother, who may have resembled him—the Crucified, whose Cross has conquered the world? Did I affirm that the stumbling block to his faith was the cornerstone of mine, and that the conformity between the Cross and the suffering of men was in my eyes the key to that impenetrable mystery whereon the faith of his childhood had perished?"

When we see suffering, when we face persecution, we have to have faith in the gospel. If you do not know the gospel, you will say God's existence is a very cruel thing. You will say the goodness of God is a cruel thing. Only faith can connect these doubts with the real world and the genuine existence of the kingdom of God. This faith does not come from us but from the gospel of Christ.

In this gospel, God tells us that he has not yet removed suffering because in this world of sin, removing suffering means ending our lives today. But through his son, through Christ on the cross, God rejects the ugliness of suffering. God does not beautify suffering, but he comes alongside people who suffer. He grants new purpose to suffering through the way of the cross.

In other words, God says to everyone who seeks him, "If your suffering is not connected with the suffering of the cross, you suffer in vain." But the suffering that is connected to the gospel of the cross will lead to a new purpose; your life will mature through the trials, giving you the hope of heavenly glory. This only comes by faith alone, through the heart of a child who has been reborn in the gospel. Only a child can trust the Lord.

God exists. And not only does he exist, he is sovereign. And not only is he sovereign, he is also good. This is what the heart of childlike faith looks like.

The person who believes by faith must be submissive and obedient like a servant. After Abel and Enoch, our passage mentions Noah, who, after being warned by God, lived in reverent fear even before anything was visible to him. In this context, "reverent fear" means after receiving something very precious, you are afraid of breaking it, so you take it and hold it very carefully.

By faith Noah did something absurd according to everyone. He used 120 years to build an ark, suffering from much ridicule and solitude. When Calvin looked at Noah, he commented that, just like water naturally flowing out of the fountain, Noah's action was obedience naturally flowing out of faith. Therefore, this is an inconceivable belief. Noah proclaims with his actions, "Today I live for a moment that has yet to come. Everything I do today is for that moment." By faith he condemned the world.

In Hebrews 11, the author does not give a perfect definition of true faith, but through eighteen examples he puts on display the faith of the saints through different generations. By faith they acted, and by faith they received the assurance and acceptance of God. This faith goes from knowledge to salvation, and this saving faith enabled these saints in the hall of faith to fully offer themselves up. They took risks, joyfully made sacrifices, and remained faithful to the end.

Therefore, today we ask God to grant this faith to everyone among us, saying, "Lord, your will be done."

Dear brothers and sisters, the churches in China have yet to go through even more difficult trials. These trials may not always be political; they may come in the form of secularism. May the gospel further disrupt the church of God and draw us by his grace.

In this difficult age, faith connects today with the future, our present life with the eternal kingdom, what we see with the unseen. With this faith in the gospel, may God help us to start a movement based on the gospel of the cross among churches in China.

Five hundred years ago, the Protestant Reformation proclaimed, "The righteous will live by faith." We "live by faith in the Son of God, who loved me and gave himself for me" (Gal. 2:20). God's promise for our faith and our life of faith is not in the past tense. In the hands of Christ our Savior, who reigns over life and death and history, everything is in the present, and he has entrusted this moment to us.

Dear brothers and sisters, this world is our monastery.

Through his Word and providence, the Spirit of God makes known to us our corruption in the flesh in order to compel us to seek shelter in him. He also manifests to us our fear of humiliation and our deep-rooted hostility against God. But faith in the gospel draws us back to him, saying, "The heart that you have received is the faith of a child." This heart of a child enables us to say, "Lord, you must become greater, I must become smaller. May your will be done. Help us, Lord. May your grace enable us to submit, to obey, and to follow. May grace grow within us, may our perseverance grow in grace, may our character grow in grace, and may our response to the mission continue to grow in grace."

"And without faith it is impossible to please him, for whoever would draw near to God must believe that he exists and that he rewards those who seek him" (Heb. 11:6).

Let those who have ears to hear say, "Amen!"

> *Dear Lord, we thank you that you gave us your holy Word, which we believe is sufficient for us.*
>
> *Lord, we believe in your holy Word, that the whole Bible bears witness to the gospel of your son, Jesus Christ.*
>
> *Lord, we know these come from your grace.*
>
> *Lord, with such grace, to whom shall we go? You have the words of eternal life. The only response we can have is to come to you like a beggar, saying, "Lord, show us your grace and mercy."*
>
> *Lord, we thank you for revealing a gospel*

*worldview to us through the Bible. Lord, when we say we walk by faith, not by sight, it is your Spirit that works in our hearts. Bring us back to that gospel worldview through which we may know the kingdom of God, our identity in the kingdom, and how we should follow you and obey you.*

*Lord, help us.*

*Lord, you are a great Savior, and all that we have before you is a humble faith, since we are only beggars from the beginning.*

*You have put faith within us, and it continues to grow.*

*Every day is your grace. Lord, by this faith we say, "Once we did not know you, but now we know you. Once we were ruled by the things we see, but today we are being ruled more and more by the invisible kingdom of the gospel. Once we were ruled by the law, but today we are compelled by the love of the cross and of the gospel."*

*Lord, transform us, guide us, and help us to hold fast to the foundation of Jesus Christ and by faith obey the one who alone rules over the universe, who alone saves us, and who not only exists but is also good.*

*We give thanks to the Lord! We pray all this in the holy name of our Lord, Jesus Christ.*

*Amen!*

## Reflect

- What is a time in your life when you needed to see "through the window" to a higher reality?

- How is knowledge of God's existence connected to having the heart of a beggar?

- How does being connected to God through faith change our experience of suffering?

- How does faith enable you to say, "Your will be done"?

# 4

# To Know the Lord

## Gao Zhen

*Gao Zhen was an early leader in the urban house churches in Beijing. He was a successful businessman before becoming a pastor, so in many ways he is a practical and proactive leader.*

*When he was first exposed to grace-centered gospel theology, he was quick to humble himself, repent and change. He is also known for his caring heart and teachability.*

Now Adam knew Eve his wife, and she conceived and bore Cain, saying, "I have gotten a man with the help of the Lord." And again, she bore his brother Abel. Now Abel was a keeper of sheep, and Cain a worker of the ground. In the course of time Cain brought to the Lord an offering of the fruit of the ground, and Abel also brought of the firstborn of his flock and of their fat portions. And the Lord had regard for Abel and his offering, but for Cain and his offering he had no regard. So Cain was very angry, and his face fell.

The Lord said to Cain, "Why are you angry, and why has your face fallen? If you do well, will you not be accepted? And if you do not do well, sin is crouching at the door. Its desire is contrary to you, but you must rule over it."

Genesis 4:1–7

My wife's first book was published last week, but I was not with her in Beijing. I met her at the airport yesterday, and she couldn't wait to give me the book and say, "Look! It just came out." I took it and flipped through it. It had nice printing and nice binding.

She insisted, "Read it."

I thought, I have so much to do, so much to read. Yet, when I finally opened it and read the first sentence of the first chapter, tears gushed out. Her book has so much to do with me. It brought me back to our love story and showed me how much our family has grown. God's grace for us did not come easily.

Many of us have a similar attitude toward the Bible today. Nice packaging, nice printing, nice binding, but what does it have to do with me? In reality, God recounts through the Bible a history that pulls every one of us into the story so that we see mankind's afflictions and the helplessness of a people mired in sin.

There is a popular song that goes, "Don't ask me where I come from; my hometown is far away. And why would I wander, wander to far places, wander." This song is saying that we don't have an answer about where we came from. It even asks why we are wandering.

Moses led the Israelites out of Egypt, and they headed to Canaan. They did not go to Canaan to have a better life. After entering Canaan, the Israelites would not eat better meat than they ate in Egypt. This is not what Moses told the Israelites. Moses wanted to tell the Israelites that they should enter Canaan as martyrs like Abel and that they should not walk in the way of Cain. The way of Cain is far from God and God's Word. In reality, deviating from God's way means entering into our self-centeredness. This is a dangerous way, a way without prospect.

Moses wrote Genesis to tell the Israelites wandering in the wilderness that their home was not far away; their home would be in Canaan. Canaan was the promised land that God had given them. Today, our life in the wilderness is a preparation for our life in Canaan. Today, our sufferings in the wilderness will be our testimony for the glory of God in Canaan.

What on earth does it mean to have a commitment to Scripture? In this passage, we see three aspects of this truth. First, it teaches us about relationships. Second, it teaches us about our work. And third, it teaches us about offering, or worship, to God. "Scripture alone" comes from relationships, the Christian life, and our worship. What Christianity cherishes is not a system of theology but that which is closely related to spiritual life.

## Vertical and Horizontal

Let us first look at relationships. "Now Adam knew Eve his wife, and she conceived and bore Cain, saying, 'I have gotten a man with the help of the Lord.' And again, she bore his brother Abel. Now Abel was a keeper of sheep, and Cain a worker of the ground." We can find many types of relationships in this paragraph. The first relationship is between husband and wife: "Adam knew Eve his wife." The second relationship is between parents and children. The third relationship is between siblings. And the fourth relationship is between humanity and the Creator.

In this passage, we find both vertical and horizontal relationships, but people in this world have only horizontal relationships. They have no vertical relationships because they reject the truth. They reject God's salvation and refuse to develop a vertical relationship with God. All they have are horizontal relationships, which are self-centered. Because they do not have this vertical relationship, the more they focus on their horizontal relationships, the more self-centered and prideful they become. Everyone wants to be the center of the world. And on a larger scale, if you look at every country's world map, they all put themselves in the center of the world. For the Chinese, there are only two countries: China (the "Middle Kingdom") and the "foreign country."[1]

But here we find an amazing relationship. When Adam and Eve were sent out of the Garden of Eden, they did not forget God's curse against them, and they did not forget God's salvation for them. They did not forget their origin, and they continued to look back to it. Therefore, Eve says, "I have gotten a man with the help of the Lord." There is a vertical relationship here between humanity and God.

Such a vertical relationship is manifested only in the hearts of Christians. Only by God's grace and salvation can it be manifested in us.

Today God has given every one of us churches so that we can develop relationships in them. The most important relationship to develop inside the church is the vertical relationship, which is not by human will—not by human flesh, not by human desire—but by God's commandments according to God's way.

The church must develop its vertical relationship with God; it should also develop horizontal relationships because God commands us to love one another. When Jesus washed the feet of the disciples, he also prayed for them and told them to serve one another. In the church we have a model to emulate—Jesus Christ, the reigning Lord.

1."Middle kingdom" is the literal translation for 中国, or "China."

However, many people come to church and do not know how to interact with other brothers and sisters. Lay leaders stare from a distance at the pastor, who is barely staying afloat. The pastor stares from a distance at the members of his congregation, who are also barely staying afloat. Our history of believing in the Lord is a history of feeling isolated and exhausted, and no one knows what to do about it. Some Christians today even refuse outright to develop relationships, trying to avoid the messiness of church life in order to showcase their unattached holiness.

How do relationships develop? Relationships start with the Triune God.

We all know that our God exists in Trinity: God the Father, God the Son, and God the Holy Spirit. Three in one and one in three; this is the internal relationship within the Godhead for all eternity. God created us in his image and likeness, putting relationships in our midst. Therefore, today we have relationships, and they come from the Triune God. First John says, "God is love." Love is a word about relationships. Life is a word about relationships. Spirituality is a word about relationships. Only in relationships can we love; only in relationships can we have life; and only in relationships can we see a person's spirituality. Christ is the head of the church, and the church is his body.

No other religions emphasize relationships. In Buddhism, I burn incense only for myself. Praying five times a day toward Mecca is to build up my own merit. Therefore, at their core, the pagan faiths are based on individualistic and self-centered solutions. When Christians do not understand this, we too become self-centered. We constantly judge others and fail to accept other people's weaknesses, and even condemn others in the name of God.

It is not about who does things better—a question that moralism is concerned with. The humbler we are in the presence of God, the more we know about God, and the more we come to realize how weak and unworthy we are.

This is what Paul said later in his life. He said, "The saying is trustworthy and deserving of full acceptance, that Christ Jesus came into the world to save sinners, of whom I am the foremost" (1 Tim. 1:15).

A pastor is not a moral model, but he should be a model for how you can follow Jesus. Therefore, Paul says, "Be imitators of me, as I am of Christ." In China and in our own churches, we need to carry a humble and repentant heart. We need to forgive our brothers and sisters. We need to accept the churches that are next to ours, and we need to stand together to serve God.

This is the first aspect of the truth—relationships.

## Constructing Our Lives

Now let us turn to the second aspect and consider our work. Over the years, numerous people have tried to defend Cain. I want to remind you that Abel chose to tend sheep, even though people did not eat meat at that time. People only began to eat meat after the ark. So there can only be one reason why Abel chose to shepherd sheep: to make an offering to God.

People may ask, How did he make a living? He had to rely on his brother. When his brother left the corners of his fields unharvested, he could glean at the corners and make a living. People with land usually had higher social status than nomads. His brother had land, while he was a nomad.

Ordinarily Chinese parents will work hard to make lots of money and leave it to their children. We want our descendants to live a better life. But many Chinese parents today do not know what it means to live a good life because there is no standard for it. If he ever considered what his descendants would do, Abel must have thought, "Cain's descendants will foster ancient civilizations, build up human society, and found nations. They will have land and cities. Yet all I have are these sheep. I will take these sheep, wander around, and find water for them to drink and grass for them to feed. What about my descendants?"

The situation in China in which we Christians live is actually a very difficult one. We face a huge challenge. Every company tries to evade their taxes, and every business demands you to do overtime. In Beijing's metro system, 9:00 p.m. is still rush hour. This is called the 9-9-6 work schedule, meaning you work from 9:00 a.m. to 9:00 p.m., six days a week. Sometimes I cannot squeeze into the metro even at 9:00 p.m. because it is still filled with young people. Therefore, Abel's mindset and motivation in choosing his occupation deserve our attention.

Let me ask you this: were people more sinful back in Abel's time, or are people more sinful today? Who is more sinful—people in the city or people in the countryside?

I have heard some people say that cities are more sinful. Just today, someone said to me, "The city is so tricky that I want to return to the countryside." And someone from Beijing once said to me, "People from Beijing have greater original sin."

It is true that few Beijing natives believe in the Lord. Most conversions in Beijing are among migrant workers. Therefore, every Chinese New Year, my church becomes empty as people go home to celebrate the holiday. Every Spring Festival, I lead short mission trips since so few people stay in town. We go to third-tier cities, and the brothers and sisters there are so passionate that they ask us to lead worship for an entire week.[2] When I go on stage there, the host reminds me to stick to the schedule, but I usually speak according to the Spirit.

But it is not an issue of the city versus the countryside. It is not an issue of this age versus Abel's age. All humans have the same sin. Men are born with the innate sin to reject truth, to reject God; they do not want to obey God. But the calling of Abel, the way of Abel, is a way of obedience to the Lord. Abel lived with the heart of martyr in this world.

Dear brothers and sisters, we Christians today cannot frivolously choose an occupation. This is God's calling for every one of us as God's children. This is our cultural commission. We cannot be associated with the world.

---

2. Chinese cities are organized and listed on a tier system according to their level of development.

Someone may ask me about what he should do. Every company he works for cheats on their taxes. I reply, "God help us! Rise up, Christian."

A sister in our church gets a two thousand yuan transportation reimbursement every month from her company. But the company has one requirement: you must submit your tickets. So, employees go to the streets and buy used tickets in order to be paid for trips they have not really taken.

One day this sister realized that this was wrong. She went to see the boss and told him, "I do not want this two thousand yuan reimbursement anymore."

The boss said, "Are you crazy?"

She said, "I am not crazy. I am a Christian. We cannot disobey God's command, because the most important mark of a Christian is to obey God's Word." She rejected the temptation.

The boss thought about it and realized, "Christians will not lie. They are honest." Although she refused the two thousand yuan monthly reimbursement, the boss promoted her in the company. She shared this story at church, saying, "Praise the Lord, halleluiah, I have overcome this temptation."

But soon another temptation came. Her mother came to Beijing and got sick, so she took her daughter's health insurance card to see the doctor. The daughter found out about it after she came home. She said, "Mom, you cannot use my insurance card. We Christians should not do these things." Her mother said, "How many Christians act like this? You are such a dumb Christian. Everyone is doing it." She still insisted, "No, you cannot use my insurance card again." Then her mother said, "If you don't let me use your insurance card, I won't go see the doctor again."

Dear brothers and sisters, God does not lead you to be covered with sin. God does not force you to follow every word he has said. But God helps you to stand firm in this age. The more Paul drew near God and knew God, the more he found himself weak and unclean. Therefore, today if you find your relationship with God increasingly comfortable, you may be at your weakest.

What does it mean that Christians are warriors? Warriors do not just raise their hands and enjoy themselves during worship. Warriors are those who take the truth and declare war against the king of this world. The king of this world speaks to you every day. He tells you that you cannot obey biblical truth; he tells you that with a little change, you will find peace.

The church that follows Scripture alone is the nobility of Christianity. The nobility is close to the emperor and faithfully carries out the emperor's decrees. In contrast, the commoners do not know the emperor's decrees. All they know is to worship the emperor. We must construct our lives around God's Word. Draw close to God, even to the point of knowing his will. Draw close to him to learn what he is revealing to you.

## Offerings to God

The third aspect to consider is our offerings to God, our worship.

Both Cain and Abel made offerings. Cain brought an offering of the fruit of the ground to the Lord, and Abel brought the firstborn of his flock and their fat portions.

Fat portions are spread all over the lamb, which makes for a whole burnt offering. The Lord had regard for Abel and his offering, but for Cain and his offering, he had no regard. So Cain became very angry, and his face fell because Cain thought God was unfair. "We both made offerings. We are brothers, and I am the older one. I am a worker of the ground. What is wrong with offering the fruit of the ground? This is what I did. I offered it to you, and you didn't like it." Then God said, "If you do well, will you not be accepted? And if you do not do well, sin is crouching at the door. Its desire is contrary to you, but you must rule over it" (Gen. 4:7). Therefore, Cain made his offering in a self-centered way.

If you want to do well, do not follow your own will. If you want to do well, obey and worship what God has revealed and live according to his way. Abel heard the voice of God; he heard stories from his parents about God, about their disobedience in the Garden of Eden, about how God saved them after they left the Garden of Eden, and about how redemption demands sacrifice and blood. Abel heard these stories and chose his occupation. He would make offerings to God for his whole life.

This age is not more sinful than Abel's age. In the presence of God, sin is always the same. Abel saw how deeply sinful he was; by himself, he could not escape judgment. He could only do that through God's salvation and by God's authority. Abel wanted to make offerings for that. But Cain lived a self-centered life. He did not care what God was saying or what God's way was.

We cannot build up a church that is far from God's way, and we cannot lead our lives according to our own feelings. We live by Scripture alone. Hallelujah!

Let us turn to Romans 8:29. "For those whom he foreknew he also predestined to be conformed to the image of his Son, in order that he might be the firstborn among many brothers." A firstborn is someone's first son. Colossians 1:15 points us to the firstborn of all creation. Jesus Christ is God's only Son; he is the only one—none before and none after him. Jesus Christ is our sole mediator.

Dear reader, what did Abel offer to God? It is the lamb that redeems. Today, we can only come into the presence of God with the precious blood of Jesus Christ, this mediator who is concealed in the Old Testament and manifested to us in the last days. Therefore, Hebrews 1:1–2 says, "Long ago, at many times and in many ways, God spoke to our fathers by the prophets, but in these last days he has spoken to us by his Son."

Jesus Christ, the Son of God, our redeemer, carried our sin on the cross, fulfilled the righteousness required by the law, and imputed this righteousness to those who believe in him. As John 3:16 says, "For God so loved the world, that he gave his only Son, that whoever believes in him should not perish but have eternal life."

*Loving God, we thank you for your precious Word again. Lord, our life cannot be built up away from your Word. Lord, we are greedy; sometimes we want to find a comfortable church for ourselves. But we also want people sitting there to hear your Word.*

*Only your Word can lead us in your way; only your way can transform our life; only your way can heal our broken hearts; only your way can remedy our relationships with our spouses; only your way can turn fathers to their children and children to their fathers.*

*Help us, Lord, so that the Chinese house churches will be built up in your way. Lord, shape the foundation of our lives and let us stand firm in the Lord our whole life.*

*Therefore, since we are surrounded by so great a cloud of witnesses, let us also lay aside every weight and sin that clings so closely, and let us run the race that is set before us, looking to Jesus, the founder and perfecter of our faith.*

*May the Spirit anoint every one of your children so that our gathering is not in vain. May your church, the church that is bought with your blood and with a heavy price.*

*We pray all these in the holy name of Jesus Christ. Amen.*

## Reflect

- How do our horizontal relationships relate to our vertical relationship with God?

- Do you think the city is more sinful than the country, or modern day more sinful than the past? What does the example of Cain and Abel teach us?

- Gao states, "If you want to do well, do not follow your own will." How does this statement fit with Gao's call for us to know the Lord?

# 5

# Jesus, the Personification of Love

## Yang Xibo

*Yang Xibo is a fourth generation Chinese Christian. His aunt was a famous evangelist named Yang Xifei who was jailed for many years. Almost every house church in Xiamen has roots in her work. He often shares that when he was growing up, he had to say he wanted to be a pastor; otherwise he had "no face" (that is, no honor) in his family. Now, he is the only one of his generation who is committed to the Christian faith.*

If I speak in the tongues of men and of angels, but have not love, I am a noisy gong or a clanging cymbal. And if I have prophetic powers, and understand all mysteries and all knowledge, and if I have all faith, so as to remove mountains, but have not love, I am nothing. If I give away all I have, and if I deliver up my body to be burned, but have not love, I gain nothing.

Love is patient and kind; love does not envy or boast; it is not arrogant or rude. It does not insist on its own way; it is not irritable or resentful; it does not rejoice at wrongdoing, but rejoices with the truth. Love bears all things, believes all things, hopes all things, endures all things.

Love never ends. As for prophecies, they will pass away; as for tongues, they will cease; as for knowledge, it will pass away. For we know in part and we prophesy in part, but when the perfect comes, the partial will pass away. When I was a child, I spoke like a child, I thought like a child, I reasoned like a child. When I became a man, I gave up childish ways. For now we see in a mirror dimly, but then face to face. Now I know in part; then I shall know fully, even as I have been fully known.

So now faith, hope, and love abide, these three; but the greatest of these is love.

1 Corinthians 13

Corinth was a coastal city in what is now Greece, the connecting point of the Achaia Peninsula. While it may have looked tiny on the map, it was a big city. It was important because it was a major transportation crossroad. Shipping goods through Corinth was three hundred nautical miles shorter than circling around the whole Achaia Peninsula. The city was a fine natural harbor for trade. It was like the coastal cities of our time, such as Shanghai or Shenzhen, where businesses flourish. A lot of wealth was accumulated there, as well as talented people. Corinth was the economic center of its time.

In his missionary journeys, Paul intentionally focused on a few urban centers: the political center, Rome; the religious center, Ephesus; the cultural center, Athens; and the economic center, Corinth. There was a popular saying in ancient Corinth, in Greece, and even across the whole Roman Empire: "Not everyone can go to Corinth." It was like what we Chinese say today: "Not everyone can go abroad or go to America." Corinth was an economically developed city, and consequently, the church there did not lack people with knowledge, talents, and gifts.

Did such human knowledge, talent, and gifts bring revival to the Corinthian church? Of course not. Paul says, "You do not lack any spiritual gift." Yet the church was full of problems. Because of their worldly sins, they brought quarreling and jealousy into the church, and they tried to solve relational problems according to worldly knowledge. As a result, they failed to govern the church according to the truth from God. They failed to settle their internal church issues and had to seek litigation among the gentiles. The knowledge, talents, and gifts of its members did not make the Corinthian church a benchmark of its day. On the contrary, it became a very corrupt and terrible church.

When we come to this chapter, we find Paul speaking as if he were one of the Corinthians—as if he has this or that gift but not love. "If I speak in the tongues of men and of angels, but have not love, I am a noisy gong or a clanging cymbal." He says that he may know all languages, from Chinese to foreign languages—English, German, Hebrew, or Greek—and he even knows the tongues of angels. But, "If I have not love, I am a noisy gong or a clanging cymbal."

In those days, the Roman world was polytheistic and, like the Chinese countryside of our time, had many temples. The priests in these temples had to make sounds with gongs and cymbals in order to attract people, and all gongs and cymbals are hollow inside so that they make sound. Paul uses this to explain that while you may have gifts and theological knowledge in the church, you are just putting on a show for yourself rather than worshiping God.

You do not love God. You are making noise, but you are empty inside. You make loud noises, but God is not interested in it.

Verse 2 says, "And if I have prophetic powers, and understand all mysteries and all knowledge, and if I have all faith, so as to remove mountains, but have not love, I am nothing." If you preach like Stephen Tong, Billy Graham, or John Sung in the 1920s and 1930s, with all prophetic power, do you think the church will revive? No! Paul says that without love, it means nothing.

You may be preaching to boost your own reputation or respect within the church, or your preaching may simply become a way to make a living. While you are doing a godly thing, you do it without love. You are still vying for power and benefit without the love of Christ. Paul says this means nothing.

We may think that if a preacher at our church knows everything being taught at all the top universities in China (Hong Kong University, Tsinghua University, and Peking University), then the church would surely revive. If you understand all the mysteries and are full of knowledge, knowing everything that is being taught in every university, that must make you an awesome evangelist. But Paul says no! Without love, the church still will not revive.

What if the preacher has all faith so as to move mountains? Or he is gifted and full of power, able to perform miracles? He can pray and heal anyone who comes to him. That would certainly make him famous.

In my city, Xiamen, there is an island called Gulangyu, and its peak is called Mount Sunlight. If I prayed tomorrow that Mount Sunlight would fly to you so you can do your devotions there, and it worked, I would certainly become the most famous preacher in the world. Many would say, "O Lord, China now has a man who can move mountains with his faith!" I believe many people would envy this power. Yet Paul says that this means nothing. If he does not have love, God may perform miracles through a man, but God is not in him. God tells us in the Bible that some of us will ask the Lord on the last day, "Did we not prophesy in your name, and cast out demons in your name?" And the Lord will reply, "I never knew you."

You ask, How can this be? How could a preacher end up like this? The Bible says it is possible. You can perform miracles, but it does not mean you are saved. Look at Judas, the traitor. When Jesus sent out the disciples two by two, they performed miracles and commanded evil spirits. Yet Judas was still lost. The Bible even says that Judas was lost from the very beginning. It is possible because the Lord looks at the heart, not at outward appearances.

If you are well trained linguistically and can speak like a teacher, then when you come to the church you may realize that you can quickly grasp the truth and knowledge that we teach at church because you already have strong language skills in the classroom. When you come to the church and share your testimony, people may be impressed because God is using your gifts, but God may not be living in you. As Jonathan Edwards mentions, gospel theology believes that the Spirit of God hovered over the face of the waters, but he would not entrust himself to water; the Spirit of God may move upon all people, but he may not live inside every one of them.

Paul has not pushed us to the corner yet, but he will. In verse 3, he says, "If I give away all I have, and if I deliver up my body to be burned, but have not love, I gain nothing." This means that I could share everything with others; I could sell my computer, my little house—everything except my wife—and donate the proceeds to the Red Cross, to missions, or to help the poor. The Bible asks, "So you think you are spiritual by doing this? You think this means God is with you?" We may think that if someone does this, his heart must be kind. But Paul says that even if you do all of this, you can still be doing it for your own benefit.

Verse 3 also mentions delivering up the body to be burned. Could such a person have no love of Christ within him? Could he still be fishing for his own benefit? Paul says it is possible.

## Human Motivations

When I am introduced to audiences, there is nothing worth mentioning except that I am Yang Xifei's nephew.

My father and uncles were all preachers who were imprisoned for the Lord. I grew up listening to testimonies from their time in prison. God was truly with them; he was real and alive. Even when they were in prison, God continued to help them with grace and righteousness. All six cousins in my extended family grew up listening to these testimonies. Not only did we not deny God's existence, we were all determined to be preachers. Whenever anyone asked any of us what we wanted to be after we grew up, we would never say a scientist or a general; that would be spiritually inferior and unthinkable in our family. You had to be a preacher in our family.

We read lots of spiritual books, including missionary testimonies of those who were martyred for the Lord in Africa. Early on I had dreams of being martyred for the Lord. I dreamed of being a missionary in Africa and spreading the gospel before being impaled by the indigenous people. Then my body would be sent back to our church, and all the brothers and sisters there would look at my body with tears and adoration and say, "Look at how much Xibo loves the Lord. He gave up everything." Then I would be in heaven looking down on earth, and I would say that the purpose of life is no more than this.

The point is that even if you think you have given up everything, it may not be for the Lord.

Dietrich Bonhoeffer says that the source of all human behavior, even the most noble of motives, is tainted with darkness. Often, when we claim that we are passionate for the Lord, we really just want to claim our own benefits and become what today we call "elite egoists."

In my study of gospel theology, Jonathan Edwards's *Religious Affections* has helped me a great deal. In this book he tells us that among all the motives in universal ethics, the deepest motivation behind everything is fear and pride. Fear means you are afraid of losing something. Pride means you want to make yourself into something. In fact, both are founded on self-centeredness and self-consideration.

Because of this, our parents know how to scare us in our childhoods. They warn us not to do bad things because the police will come after us. They use fear to correct our behavior. Then when you attend kindergarten, the teacher introduces both physical punishment and a reward system. The teacher gives you a red star because you did something good today. I was deeply troubled as a kid because I was too naughty to earn any red stars. I envied other kids who had lots of stars, sometimes even two lines of them. I wanted to behave better so I could get some red stars.

Then we grow up, and we do not cheat for two reasons. One is that if I ever got caught cheating, I would be embarrassed. Yes, you may look honest and refuse to cheat, but the motive behind it may be fear or pride. I despised those classmates who cheated, and I wanted to tell them that I could do it by myself. I wanted to be different from them; I wanted to stand out. Fear and pride stay with us even when we start working as we begin to worry about pay cuts and perfect attendance bonuses. Fear and pride are both issues of self-centeredness.

There is a top philanthropist in China who is known for donating his wealth to others. Once I was watching a Taiwanese TV program about him donating money in Taiwan. A local anchor came to interview him. She asked him, "What are you are doing this for? You were the first to donate to the 2008 Sichuan earthquake recovery. You have already donated a lot of money, and now you are donating money in Taiwan. Why?" He replied, "Nothing. I plan to keep on giving until I die. I want to give away everything to the poor after I die." He was willing to do high-profile philanthropy and said that, like a bully who does bad things forcefully, he wanted to be someone who does good things forcefully.

# Jesus, the Personification of Love

The reporter kept asking him why he did good things. He finally admitted that in his childhood, he felt the joy of doing good and wanted to keep doing it. "Because in my childhood I helped a classmate, and the teacher gave me a red star on my face. I was so happy that I kept it on my face the whole week. Every time it fell off, I put it back on right away. And because I do good things now, I ask everyone around to watch me closely. If I go to the massage parlor or any other sex establishment, anyone who catches me will be rewarded one million yuan. Consequently, I am very cautious when I leave home because so many people are watching me. I can only relax when I come home."

The reporter kept asking for more reasons. Then he told her about the first thing he did in Taiwan. He said, "I loved Deng Lijun," who was a famous Taiwanese singer. "So, I visited her tomb. When I was at the tomb, there were fresh bouquets of flowers. People are still thinking of her today." He said, "What do I want? All I want is that after I die, someone would write on my tomb, 'XXX, the great, good man of China.'" I say that he is still worldly and self-centered; pride and fear are still the motivations behind everything he does.

Are Christians like this?

If we reflect on ourselves, we are just as unable to leave fear and pride behind. I grew up in a Christian family, and our home was where the church met. Before we gathered for worship, my aunt and my father would ask me to set up the chairs. I would do it. But if I did it alone, I would become upset and wonder, Where are my cousins? Why do I have to do this alone?

But then if the elderly sisters and brothers praised me saying, "Xibo, you are so spiritual and so mature at such a young age," I would work diligently and never miss any gatherings. I remember that we would have at least three or four gatherings every week, and that was considered infrequent. I did not dare miss any of them. I was afraid God would tell me that I would fail my exam the next week because I missed the gatherings; therefore, I attended those gatherings diligently. In this world, fear and pride stimulate us by appealing to our self-centeredness and our focus on our own benefit.

Oftentimes when we forget the love of Christ and come to the church, we are in fact doing the very same thing. We do not have confidence in Christ, and we become fearful; we are afraid that our current disobedience will bring future punishment from God. If we encounter suffering, we say all of our previous good deeds were not rewarded, and God does not really exist. We are still concerned only about our own benefit.

## Love Is a Person

Paul understands the human heart. He says that through all our pious activity, we are still seeking our own benefit. Therefore, starting in verse 4, Paul says, "Love is patient and kind; love does not envy or boast; it is not arrogant or rude. It does not insist on its own way; it is not irritable or resentful; it does not rejoice at wrongdoing, but rejoices with the truth. Love bears all things, believes all things, hopes all things, endures all things. Love never ends."

# Jesus, the Personification of Love

We are very familiar with this passage, and yet we are still capable of looking at it without being Christ-centered. We can read it as if it were only a moral standard. I am not saying that we do not need moral standards. God's law is holy, and his law is the moral standard. We do need it, but our salvation does not come from this moral standard. You are saved because of the love of God, because Jesus Christ died for us on the cross, because he fully offered himself. You are not saved by your obedience.

If you take this passage only as a moral standard, those of us who have been serving the church for a long time know that these words can be used to attack others in an argument. "He does not love me enough because he is not patient with me. He always counts my wrongdoings. He always brings up the old scores." We use these words to protect ourselves rather than living them out ourselves.

However, in the original text, there is no verb "is." In Greek, the noun "love" is the subject with a verb right after it. So a more accurate translation would be, "Love lies in patience; love contains kindness; love does not envy; love does not boast; love is not arrogant." That is to say, this love is not a worldly, abstract kind of love; it is personal.

I was familiar with this passage even in my childhood, but I was scared to boast about it to my friends. We were beginning to study literature, and I soon found out that no one in the world describes love like this. When we treat love as a noun, we describe it like ice cream in the summer or like fire in the winter; a breathtaking or heart-warming love. When you describe love, because it is a noun, you describe it with scenarios. What is love? Love is like an elderly couple holding hands together in the sunset. What is love? Love is like a baby in a mother's arms. When you talk like this, people think you are very good with words.

When I was young, I believed that if I told my classmates, "Love does not envy; it is not resentful or irritable; love does not boast," they might think my Christian literature was just average. In fact, Paul's theology is inseparable from Jesus. First Corinthians uses the gospel of Christ to solve all the problems in the Corinthian church, and we treat the book as a manual for church problems. But in this love chapter, Paul is actually describing a personified love. Who does Paul think could personify this type of love? It is Jesus.

Substitute the word *love* with *Jesus*, and you will find that it reads quite smoothly. Observe: "Jesus is patient and kind; Jesus does not envy or boast; Jesus is not arrogant or rude. Jesus does not insist on his own way; Jesus is not irritable or resentful; Jesus does not rejoice at wrongdoing, but rejoices with the truth. Jesus bears all things, believes all things, hopes all things, endures all things." You can feel that this passage was intended to describe a personal God who endures for us, believes in us, treats us with kindness, never boasts, and always comforts us.

Jesus is often relegated to simply a moral model. I am not saying that Jesus cannot be a moral model, because the Bible tells us to imitate Christ. But before you imitate

Christ, before you are sanctified, you must know that Jesus Christ truly died for you as a free gift of grace. You must understand this in order to be sanctified; otherwise your sanctification is self-reliant and self-centered, and self-centeredness is the source of all sin. If Jesus Christ is only our model, I can tell you right now that there is no way we can imitate him. He said that we should love our enemies. When he was on the cross, he said, "Father, forgive them, for they know not what they do."

My first name is Xibo, named after the book of Hebrews. But my classmates would call me A Po (meaning "old lady") or Xi Gua ("watermelon"). I would get really angry, but I could not fight with them, so I would go home and complain to my parents. My father was a preacher, and he asked me to forgive them. They did not know what they were doing, and I should forgive them.

I complained to my parents a few more times before I started to argue with them. I would say, "There is no way I can forgive them!" My father would say, "Do you know Jesus died on the cross for his enemies?" I would respond, "He is God, and I am a man. I cannot forgive them; only God can." If you treat Jesus only as a moral model, you are just like the Indian Mahatma Gandhi, who always carried the Sermon on the Mount in his pocket but refused to recognize Jesus as the Savior.

# An Ethic of Gratitude

Fear and pride stand behind all universal ethics. But there is another type of ethic from the gospel that can free us from both, and that is thanksgiving. One of my co-workers told me a story that explains the ethics behind the gospel, and I have shared it on many occasions. There is a river with many people walking next to it. You and I walk by it all the time. Someone falls into the river, and I say, "Oh no! Someone fell into the river, but it is too dangerous to rescue him." Then I see Jesus jump in and save him, bringing him back to the bank. All of a sudden, I become very passionate because I realize there is someone in this world who willingly sacrifices his life to save others, and he has died after rescuing another. I say, "What a highly moral person to sacrifice himself to save others."

But the gospel is not about you seeing Jesus jump in to save others; it is not about other people falling into the river. The gospel is about us falling into the river ourselves, and Jesus jumping in to save us. If you only treat Jesus as a role model for saving others, next time someone falls into the river and Jesus is not around, you jump in and save that person. He thanks you, and you say in your heart, "You are welcome." But you really feel in the depth of your heart, "I am almost as great as Jesus is. At least after I saved him, I am still alive. I must be great."

But the ethic of the gospel is that you yourself fell into the river, and when you fell, Christ sacrificed his life and saved you. When someone else falls in, you stop struggling with the question of whether you should save him, because you have received an amazing grace. When you do save him, you point elsewhere when he says, "Thank you." You know that by your nature, you have no power to save him. Sacrifice is not in our nature; only self-love is. But because Christ saved me, I can now save you so that you may come to know him. Jesus's salvation rescues us not only from the authority of hell but also from the authority of sin so that we can continue to witness his redemption and salvation.

Let me tell you a story about an elderly sister, because I know Christ lives in her. This elderly sister is in our church. She will be ninety-three this year. I often visit the homes of our senior members with brothers and sisters. We have a program that asks brothers and sisters who are willing to take the challenge to serve in the church for a full year to determine whether they are fit for full-time ministry. Visiting senior members is one of their tasks.

This elderly sister took out her Bible when we were visiting her that morning. Every morning, she would get up early to read the Bible and devotional books. My father and my aunt would recommend devotions to her, and she would wrap the books with book covers and change them every year. There were many marks on the Bible, showing that she had read it through many times. There were marks on the Bible showing the years and months that she finished reading it through. Every morning, she would get up at 4:00 a.m. to pray, cook breakfast, and then pray again with her husband. And then she would go serve the church with two other sisters who are both in their eighties.

Every week they would take buses into Xiamen and go visit elderly people in various nursing homes and hospitals because these people were too old to come to church. When I went out to visit other people with her, I would worry about her, because her breathing was very heavy. She would become short of breath whenever we went up the stairs, as if she were about to lose it totally. I worried about her a lot at the beginning.

But she would tell me not to worry about her. When she was young, she was beaten in the Cultural Revolution for being a lackey of imperialism. Her lungs were damaged, and then she developed lung cancer as she got older. She has only one airway for breathing, so she would fight for air every time she breathed. I was afraid to visit others with her for fear that her family would cause me trouble if she died on the road. But she would tell me not to worry. It would be better to die on the road serving the Lord than to die at home.

One day we were going to visit others, and she had to put a comforter into a cabinet. She prayed to the Lord and said, "Lord, I could fall and die, but please do not let me fall and suffer from fractures, because it would cause my family a lot of trouble to take care of me; rather, if I must fall, let me die and be with you."

When she was ninety, one morning she got up with a mini-stroke and was sent to the hospital. Her family called me about the mini-stroke. I rushed to the hospital, and the doctor had just arrived. Her nephew arranged a nice VIP room for her. When the doctor came, he took some time to speak with her, and then she said, "I think my time is up, and I am about to leave this world. I have nothing to worry about since my whole family believes in the Lord. So it would be good for me to go to the Lord."

The doctor heard this and thought, This elderly lady doesn't want to live anymore. She has no hope. So he immediately said, "Ma'am, you've got to live with some hope." I almost fell on the ground: you just asked this ninety-year-old lady to live with hope? She has no hope except to see the Lord soon.

Once I took the members of our ministry training program to visit a preacher in the countryside. A church of about a dozen people meets in his home. We worshiped there, and I preached. Afterward I invited the preacher to speak to us, and he did. He said, "I did not tell you earlier that I am actually building a house. Everyone in the village is laughing at me because I have two sons, both of whom are now serving the Lord as preachers. One is going to the frontier far away, the other one is in the nearby countryside. So, I have no children close to me."

He went on to say, "I built this current house when I was young. Now this house is old and shabby. I am too old to build a new house, and my children cannot come to help me. People laugh at me because I have to do it by myself. So, I keep praying. One time the workers told me that there were not enough bricks for the day, and I could not carry more bricks in by myself. So, I prayed to the Lord, and then a brother came to visit me, and we both went out to get the bricks. On the way, we met a relative who helped with the bricks as well."

He said, "You see, how faithful God is! When I was in trouble, I cried out to him, and Christ did not disappoint me."

It was a few weeks after Christmas, and he said one thing that night that deeply touched me. He said that Christmas is all about God sending his son into the world for us. He said, "Since God gave his son for me, I would love to give my two sons to him, because God would give his son for me."

It was the first time I heard someone explain Christmas to me in this way—"God gave his son for me"—and I was deeply moved. If I have children in the future, I will also give my children to God the way he did. Lord, help me.

Recently, I have been reading a book by David Martyn Lloyd-Jones, who says that historians believe that if the Puritans had not gone into the English countryside to change that backward culture by building schools and churches, England could still be stuck in superstition and spirit worship. Because of Puritans like David Martyn Lloyd-Jones who went to serve in fishing villages, England was transformed.

I have seen the needs of many house churches in China. We are rich, even richer than the Corinthian church of its time. But I still see that many churches continue to gather and worship with just a few people. How many young people—how many brothers and sisters among us—would go like the Puritans to remote areas that need their service?

I can only ask God to fill us with love.

*Lord, we thank you!*

*We come to your presence knowing that we constantly neglect this magnificent salvation; we constantly neglect your love for us; we constantly neglect your ongoing forgiveness and protection toward us; we constantly neglect that your love for us is filled with patience; and we constantly neglect that love is not without truth. Lord, we are so easily overcome by this world.*

*Lord, may your love be known to us. Show yourself to us, awaken our hearts, and fill us with power to respond to your love. Thank you!*

*We pray in the holy name of our Lord, Jesus Christ. Amen.*

## Reflect

- Think of a church that exemplified the Christian life to you. What made it memorable?

- What gifts or skills are you tempted to associate with spiritual maturity more than love?

- What difference would it make in your faith to understand love as a person rather than an idea?

# Conclusion: The Gospel Grows in China

Over the course of four days in May 2017, nearly three thousand mainland house church pastors, leaders, and laypeople gathered in Hong Kong to worship and learn together at an event called "Reformation 500 and the Gospel." At this convention, many of the house church's leading pastors, such as Wang Yi and Gao Zhen, shared the stage with respected American theologians—John Piper, Paul David Tripp, and Richard Pratt. It was a historic moment for the church in China.

Though the size of the event was significant for the house church, size was only part of what amazed attendees and observers alike. The truly remarkable aspect of the event was that it had not been organized by an outside, foreign organization. A first for modern house church history, the convention had been planned, executed, and financed largely by Chinese churches working together in a single, indigenous movement. The vision behind the convention was a testimony to the growing maturity of the house church—not only in resources and theology but in hearts bent toward unity.

For decades following the communist revolution in China, Christians met in small gatherings in personal homes, hence the term *house church*; however, in the past twenty years, house church has in many ways become no more than a traditional term for churches that now commonly rent commercial space for their weekly meetings, post sermons online for anyone to hear, and host large evangelistic events in public parks. Due to these churches' continued refusal to submit to the government's desire for ecclesiastical authority, a more technically correct term would be *unregistered church*. Despite the nuances of terminology, 家庭教会, or "house church," remains the chosen identity.

For those familiar with the Chinese house church, seeing the cooperation required for Reformation 500 points to changing attitudes among what were once churches controlled by suspicion and distrust. Historically, China's house churches have been divided, either unaware of each other's presence or unwilling to build the trust necessary for cooperation, leaving churches scattered haphazardly across cities. Reformation 500 loudly proclaimed a shift toward unity and an emboldening of the house church's identity.

What brought the Chinese house church to this moment?

The short answer is that a gospel movement called Grace to the City has been sweeping across the traditional Chinese house church, calling churches back to the historic gospel of grace as they live and exist in China's new urban centers.

## The Story of a Gospel Movement

*Movement* is a tricky word for the Chinese. **运动** typically connotes something especially big and particularly political. In English, a movement is something that can be big or small, and the word is commonly tossed around in church contexts for any new initiative taking place. But for the Chinese, *movement* belongs to such historic events as the student democracy movement, which led to the June 4 event at Tiananmen Square, or President Xi Jiping's current anti-corruption campaign.

And this is what Grace to the City is explicitly *not*.

From the beginning, Grace to the City has been a quiet theological and ministry movement. Its focus is on the church, God's people, and orthodox faith. It is not a movement in the Chinese sense of the word but rather an effort to build up faithful, biblical churches.

In the midst of China's great urban boom, many house churches found themselves transitioning from being primarily rural to urban, and their leaders discovered they did not know how to engage the city. While considering this problem, a number of Chinese house church leaders met with American pastor Timothy Keller in 2009, an initial relationship that led to seventeen Chinese house church leaders going to New York for one month of training a year later. These pastors came from Beijing, Shanghai, Xiamen, and Chengdu, as well as the more rural areas of Henan and Anhui Provinces.

# Conclusion

They were surprised to discover the month in New York City was not about learning a method; it was about understanding a core gospel theology. Church planting methods were not the focus but instead an outflow based on this gospel-centric theology.

Some of these pastors deeply connected with the training. Their theology became fresh and was flipped inside-out. Many spoke of a new ability to see their works-based, legalistic tendencies as they personally experienced a revived understanding of grace. These pastors perceived and appreciated that the core value of what they received was not a method but rather a fresh perspective on how to think theologically, how to approach ministry, how to interpret and align everything with Scripture. They grew in their understanding that church planting is not about a method but rather about the gospel, and they helped form the seed of what would later become Grace to the City.

They began to travel to China's cities, training pastors in gospel theology. All sorts of different house church or denominational leaders came into the movement, attracted by its gospel emphasis. The movement was Chinese-led from the start.

Focusing on grace is a major paradigm shift for many churches in China. As one leader of Grace to the City has said, "The traditional Chinese house church thinks, 'Who are those guys? What are they talking about? They are not pious enough.'" But the main questions Grace to the City is asking are, What is the gospel? And, What is the church?

And those two really come down to just one fundamental question, namely, Who is Christ?

Christianity has only taken root in the Chinese context for a little more than 150 years, so the church is still young and swayed by theological trends. Like so many churches, the house church can use piety or doctrine to replace Christ himself and fail to point to Christ and have union with him.

In Chinese culture you have both extreme legalism and antinomianism (flagrant disregard for God's law). Daoism talks about freedom—personal freedom, outer freedom, nobody constraining you. And to some extent even Confucianism strives to achieve a final state of freedom. Initially, when you share the gospel and the law of God, Chinese people hate any restriction from religion.

And yet to some extent, they are also very legalistic. Deep in the hearts of Chinese people is the Confucian idea that achieving personal social status comes through public morality. Religion is also something they can use, both consciously and unconsciously, to build up their own status. Deep in their hearts, though, they do not want to obey God's law. They do not like it. Everybody, in his or her heart, is like the prodigal son. Like all peoples, grace is not in our blood.

So the fundamental challenge is truly comprehending grace. The only solution is to talk about the person of Christ and what God has been doing. It is not a matter of finding the balance between grace and law; it is a matter of finding a person, Christ.

# Why the City?

The biblical idea of the city is entirely different from our common, human understanding of the city. In addition, the way the West talks about the city is different from how the Chinese talk about the city.

The Western concept of the city was built up through Greek and Roman thought. In the ancient Greco-Roman world, rural areas were for the barbarians, and the cities were civilized. This maintained its influence until the early stages of the Protestant missionary movement so that missionaries went primarily into the cities.

However, in China the rural areas were the more civilized place for two thousand years. Now modern society has flipped this around. The rural areas are dramatically declining and decaying, and the urban areas are booming. Everyone wants to go to the cities. For the Chinese, this is a dramatic and abrupt transformation of the concept of the city.

As a result, Grace to the City not only needs to deal with questions concerning true grace, but it also must ask questions about the city. Given China's intense and rapid urbanization, the theology developing among China's pastors is opening up a new biblical eschatology of the city.

The deepest meaning of a city in the Bible points to the corporate community of humanity. In Genesis 1, Scripture tell us that God rested after his labor of creation. Where did he rest? He rested in the Garden of Eden, where humanity had been created. That deep union, that communion of

God with created humanity, is the basic idea of the city. The author of Psalm 46 says that there is a river coming out of God's throne that makes the city rejoice. And even the new Jerusalem, the eventual city, is a church, a corporate humanity.

At its core, the city is newly created humanity. This is the eschatological aim of Grace to the City.

S. E. Wang

# About the Editors

**S. E. Wang** is the president of China Partnership, where he works to serve a gospel-centered movement focused on church planting and pastoral training in the urban centers of China. He is also the Cofounder and Director of Theological Content for the Center for House Church Theology. A fifth generation Christian from Beijing, China, he received his PhD in computer science at Michigan State and a Master of Arts in Religion from Westminster Theological Seminary in Philadelphia.

**Hannah Nation** is the Director of Content for China Partnership and the Cofounder and Managing Director for the Center for House Church Theology. She is a research associate at Gordon-Conwell's Center for the Study of Global Christianity, and has written for The Gospel Coalition and Christianity Today. She received her Master of Arts in Church History from Gordon-Conwell Theological Seminary.

**CHINA PARTNERSHIP**

To find out more about how you can pray for, encourage, and learn about China, follow us at
**ChinaPartnership.org**

Made in the USA
Columbia, SC
01 April 2021